the merging
of diverse,
distinct,
or separate
elements
into a
unified
whole

Water \ˈwȯ tər\ n.:
a theme throughout Scripture

by Chad Bird

CONCORDIA PUBLISHING HOUSE • SAINT LOUIS

Author: Chad Bird
Editor: Mark Sengele
Design: Karol Bergdolt

Your comments and suggestions concerning the material are appreciated.
Please write the Editor of Youth Materials, Concordia Publishing House, 3558 S. Jefferson Avenue,
St. Louis, MO 63118-3968

This publication may be available in braille or large print or on cassette tape for the visually impaired.
Please allow 8 to 12 weeks for delivery. Write to the Library for the Blind, 1333 S. Kirkwood Road,
St. Louis, MO 63122–7295; call 1-800-433-3954, ext. 1322; or e-mail to blind.library@lcms.org.

Manufactured in the United States of America

TABLE OF CONTENTS

INTRODUCTION

About the Fusion Series

Fusion—the merging of diverse, distinct, or separate elements into a unified whole. Fusion is a word that speaks of energy and excitement, whether you are talking about a style of music or a nuclear reaction.

God's Word is filled with fusion. The Old Testament bears many hints of events to come in the New Testament, yet we often miss the connection. The *Gospel message* of the Savior is seen time and time again in the Old Testament. Through this series you will come to connect—fuse—those events and messages for yourself and your participants.

Each study in the Fusion Series gathers stories from Scripture—both Old and New Testaments—around a common theme. Through the study of that theme we pray that you come to a deeper understanding of the Gospel message of Jesus Christ as Lord and Savior.

Fusion—Water

Almost every page of the Old Testament is wet. It is amazing to observe how often water finds its way into OT stories, especially stories about how God is at work to bless or save His people. From the opening words in Genesis to the closing words of the prophets, we continually hear about how God joins His Word of grace to water. He uses it to lift up the ark to carry Noah and his family to safety; He uses it at the Red Sea to rescue His people, Israel, from the murderous pursuit of Pharaoh; He brings it out of a rock in the wilderness to demonstrate to Israel that He is the God who brings life out of death. By the time you get to the New Testament, it comes then as no surprise when God "in the flesh," Jesus Christ, chooses water as the element of creation by which to save sinners and bring them into His life-giving body. Holy Baptism has been hinted at all along.

Using These Materials

Fusion Series Bible studies are designed to challenge your participants to develop a deeper knowledge and understanding of Scripture. These studies are designed to work for a large-group presentation or a small-group Bible study. While there are six sessions outlined in the book, we have not suggested a time frame for each section of the lesson. The level of participant interest, discussion, and further questions will help establish the length of time spent on each section. This flexibility also allows you to use this material for more than six one-hour sessions. You can easily adapt this material to 12 or more hour-long lessons.

Each session contains reproducible participant pages. These pages may be given to participants as you work through the lesson together in class. As an alternative, you may give copies of these pages to participants in advance of the session so that they may complete their personal study before coming to class.

The leader materials work through the questions from the participant pages and provide additional commentary and insights for the Bible class leader. You will want to study these notes as you prepare to lead each session.

It is assumed that the Bible class leader will have the usual basic equipment and supplies available—pencils or pens for each participant and a chalkboard or its equivalent (whiteboard, overhead transparency projector, or newsprint pad and easel) with corresponding markers or chalk. Encourage the participants to bring their own Bibles. Then they can mark useful passages and make notes to guide their personal Bible study and reference. Do provide additional Bibles, however, for visitors or participants who do not bring one. The appropriate participant pages should be copied in a quantity sufficient for the class.

1

CREATION

Lesson Focus

As you walk through the story of creation, you keep getting your feet wet. There's water all over the place! The account is virtually flooded with this liquid. What is important to see is what God does with water. How is He linked with the water? What does He join to the water or separate from the water? How does He use water to bless His creation, in particular, His most beloved of creatures—Adam and Eve?

Opening Prayer

Father in heaven, as at the baptism in the Jordan River You once proclaimed Jesus Your beloved Son and anointed Him with the Holy Spirit, grant that all who are baptized in His name may faithfully keep the covenant into which they have been called, boldly confess their Savior, and with Him be heirs of life eternal; through Jesus Christ, who lives and reigns with You and the Holy Spirit, one God, now and forever. Amen (Collect for the Baptism of Our Lord, *Lutheran Worship,* p. 21).

Water, Water Everywhere

Ask students to name as many uses of water as they can think of. (Drinking, washing, swimming, cooling off, and so forth.)

Have students name some biblical stories, from the Old Testament or New Testament, that involve water in some way. What common elements draw these stories together?

Almost every page of the Old Testament is wet. It is amazing to observe how often water finds its way into Old Testament stories, especially stories about how God is at work to bless or save His people. From the opening words in Genesis to the closing words of the prophets, we continually hear how God joins His Word of grace to water. He uses it to lift up the ark to carry Noah and his family to safety; He uses it at the Red Sea to rescue His people, Israel, from the murderous pursuit of Pharaoh; He brings it out of a rock in the wilderness to demonstrate to Israel that He is the God who brings life out of death. By the time you get to the New Testament, it comes then as no surprise when God "in the flesh," Jesus Christ, chooses water as the

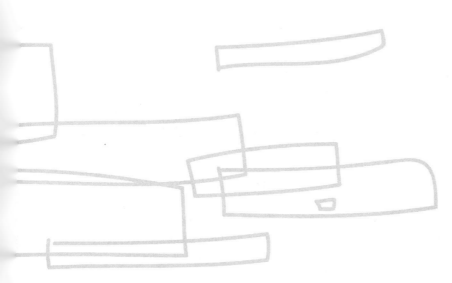

element of creation by which to save sinners and bring them into His life-giving body. Holy Baptism has been hinted at all along.

In the Beginning . . . Everything Was Wet!

Read Genesis 1 and 2. Locate all the verses that mention water.

How does God interact with creation? Is He pictured as distant or close, involved or uninvolved? What does this tell us about God's relationship with creation?

God's various uses of water in Genesis 1 prepare us to hear of how God takes water in hand later in the biblical story to accomplish His great acts of salvation. Already here at the beginning, one thing is certain: God is not ashamed to get His hands wet! He is the Creator who is not aloof from His creation. He is not a hands-off Deity with no desire to be involved intimately with the things He has created. Rather, in those very elements of creation, God our Father is profoundly present: to sustain, to uphold,

to bless, to save. He is our sacramental Father; the God who wraps Himself in the lowly stuff of creation so that we, His creatures, might find Him there.

Day 1: The Spirit of God and Water

Which persons of the Trinity are explicitly mentioned in the first two verses of Genesis 1?

Compare Genesis 1:1–5 with 2 Peter 3:1–7. Out of what does Peter say the earth was formed? What does that tell you about the prominence of water in the creation account?

In the beginning God created the heavens and the earth, and the heavens and the earth were saturated with water. Before the sun and moon existed, before dirt and animals, before man and woman, there was a creation soaked with water. This water united. It united the earth. It united the earth and the heavens. It united all creation, for it was literally everywhere. In fact, one can almost say that everything that now is, started out "in infancy" as water! St. Peter puts it this way: "The heavens existed long ago, and the earth was formed *out of water and through water* by the word of God" (2 Peter 3:5, emphasis added). "Out of water and through water"—that says it all. It was the fundamental element of creation. Although God created the heavens and the earth out of nothing (*ex nihilo*, as theologians say), He created many things from the elements of creation He had already made. It was sort of a two-step process. First He made dust, and then from that dust (step 1) He made Adam. From Adam's rib, He made Eve. Since God created earth "out of water and through water," we could use the language of the Small Catechism to confess, "I believe that God has made me and all creatures *out of water.*"

Where is the Spirit, and what is He doing? Would it be correct to say that the Spirit is also the Creator, along with the Father? What does the Nicene Creed say about the Spirit in this regard?

Why might it be that the Spirit is described as "moving" or "fluttering"? With what bird is the Spirit later associated?

Over the watery mass of creation hovered the Spirit of God. "The earth was without form and void, and darkness was over the face of the deep. And the Spirit of God was hovering over the face of the waters" (Genesis 1:2). The Hebrew word translated as "hovering" (*rachaph*) is specifically the "hovering" associated with wings (compare Deuteronomy 32:11, where the eagle "hovers" or "flutters" [*rachaph*] over her young). So the Spirit of God was "hovering" or "fluttering" over the surface of the waters.

First, notice that God is present at creation in His Spirit. He is not way, way up in heaven somewhere beaming down commands to the far-off earth. No, He is right there, almost getting wet! *Second,* notice that He is called "the Spirit of God." The Spirit, who would later descend upon the apostles at Pentecost, was there from the beginning, actually, before the beginning. He is the Spirit who

proceeds from the Father and the Son from all eternity. As the second-century church father St. Irenaeus would later say, God our Father created the heavens and the earth with His two "hands"—the Son and the Spirit. There fluttering above the water is one of those "hands," the hand of the Spirit.

Third, notice that the Holy Spirit is depicted with wings, like a dove. And how fitting this is! For when Jesus was baptized, the Holy Spirit descended upon Him in the form of a dove (Matthew 3:16). Needless to say, this was no mere coincidence! The very same Spirit that hovered like a dove over the first creation now hovered over Jesus when He was baptized in the water of creation. The Spirit who was present to create the earth "out of water and through water" was there on Jesus to create everything anew. He came to form a new creation in Jesus Christ out of the water of His baptism and by means of the water of His baptism. As Paul says, "For as many of you as were baptized into Christ have put on Christ" (Galatians 3:27) and "If anyone is in Christ, he is a new creation. The old has passed away; behold, the new has come" (2 Corinthians 5:17).

Read Genesis 1:1–5 in light of Matthew 3:16 and 2 Corinthians 5:17. In what way is the Spirit present at Jesus' baptism and at our Baptism? What does the Spirit create at Baptism?

This same Spirit who hovered over the first waters of the old creation, who hovered over and landed upon Jesus at the new creation in His baptism, now also hovers over every baptismal font in which sinners are created anew in Jesus. He hovers over every baptismal font to fill that water with the creating, saving Word of Jesus. He washes sinners into the new creation made flesh—the body of Jesus. Here sins are washed away. Here there is a re-genesis as the Spirit fills young and old with the life of Jesus.

Day 2: The Expanse and Separation

Read Genesis 1:6–8. Describe what happened on the second day of creation.

On the first day of creation God began His work of separation. He separated the light from the darkness. On the second day of creation this separation continued. He said, "Let there be an expanse . . ." (Genesis 1:6). The heavens and the earth, once united in water and by means of water, are no longer one but two. In the Hebrew picture of creation, the "firmament" (KJV) was like a huge oval dam that held back the waters above from flooding onto the earth below.

Read Genesis 7:11–12 and 2 Peter 3:6. Where does much of the water come from in these verses? Was the original water of creation designed by God for such punishment? Is then creation also affected by human sin? How?

From this firmament flowed the killing waters of the Flood in Noah's day (Genesis 7:11–12). Water fell from above onto a creation that had corrupted itself. Peter links the creation "out of water and through water" with this destruction by water: "and that by means of these the world that then existed was deluged with water and perished" (2 Peter 3:6)

After Noah there was yet another flood that flowed from heaven—not a flood of water but of wrath. The divine wrath of God for our sins flooded down upon the Son of God as He hung on the cross. His body was like the earth, flooded with the waters of divine punishment. He was all creation reduced to one, every sinner reduced to one, drowned in the waves of punishment for everyone's iniquity.

But now that Christ has reconciled heaven to earth, now that He has been flooded with divine wrath and been raised again, water has been transformed. It has become for us the means by which we, who are of the earth, are joined to heaven. At the baptismal font heaven and earth are once again united in water. As at Jesus' baptism, when the heavens were opened (Matthew 3:16), so at our Baptism the heavens are open, the firmament is split. But instead of wrath flowing down, the fatherly voice of love speaks, saying, "You, O baptized child, are My beloved child. In you I am well-pleased, for you are in My Son, Jesus." Wet with the water of the new creation, we are born again as earthly children of our heavenly Father.

Day 3: Gathering of Waters into Seas

Read Genesis 1:9–13. How would you summarize the work on God on the third day of creation?

On the third day of creation God separated the dry land from water. "And God said, 'Let the waters under the heavens be gathered together into one place, and let the dry land appear.' And it was so" (Genesis 1:9). As on Day 2, when He separated the water of the heavens from the water of the earth, now He separated the dry land from water. The purpose of this separation was the creation of life on land. "And God said, 'Let the earth sprout vegetation, plants yielding seed, and fruit trees bearing fruit in which is their seed, each according to its kind, on the earth.' And it was so. The earth brought forth vegetation, plants yielding seed according to their own kinds, and trees bearing fruit in which is their seed, each according to its kind. And God saw that it was good" (Genesis 1:11–12). The vegetation and fruit trees were to serve as food for the animals, as well as for the man and woman who would be created on the sixth day.

When God creates these seas, He demonstrates that He sets certain bounds upon creation. As He asks Job, "Who shut in the sea with doors when it burst out from the womb?" (Job 38:8). Like a baby in its playpen, the sea is confined, prevented from crawling all over the surface of the earth.

What adjectives come to mind when you think of the sea: calm or troubled, safe or dangerous, peaceful or violent?

Read Psalms 18:16; 46:2–3; 65:7; 69:1–2, 14–15; 89:9. How did the people of Israel think of the sea? How does this compare with your picture of the sea?

This confinement of the sea was, for Israel, direct testimony to the power of God over chaos and discord. For the people of old, the sea was not the picture of calm serenity. It was the icon of tumult, confusion, death, and violence. In fact, in many of the psalms the enemies of Israel were compared to seas or waters that attacked with wave after wave of violence. Thus, when God, by His Word, put a boundary to the sea, He put up a boundary that was for the good of His people.

Read Matthew 8:23–27. How is Jesus' action in the boat similar to what God did in Genesis 1?

When Jesus was crossing the Sea of Galilee with His disciples, a great storm swept down upon those waters (Matthew 8:23–27). While the disciples tried with all their might to keep the boat afloat, Jesus slept. Finally, when the hopes of the disciples were dashed by the mighty waves, they woke up Jesus and begged Him to help. Jesus arose and rebuked the winds and the sea. A great calm came over the waters. It was like Genesis 1—only better. There stood the Creator, looking out over the roaring sea. By a mere word from His mouth, He overcame the chaos and discord. Where there was impending death—came life and peace. The disciples were amazed, and rightly so, for they had just seen a reenactment of Genesis 1. There stood God, in their boat!

Read Revelation 20:13–21:1. The sea is mentioned twice in these verses. Is it described in positive or negative terms? With what is the sea compared in Revelation 20:13? Why will there be no sea in heaven?

In St. John's Revelation, God gives him a vision of the new creation. In this beautiful description of the new heavens and the new earth there is one missing element that initially strikes us as strange: there is no longer any sea. "Then I saw a new heaven and a new earth, for the first heaven and the first earth had passed away, and the sea was no more" (Revelation 21:1).

Now we know why! In this place of perfection, where God reigns in perfect peace over His perfected creation, there is no place for discord, confusion, death, and violence. Indeed, just a few verses before chapter 20, John likened the sea to a huge graveyard: "And the sea gave up the dead who

were in it, Death and Hades gave up the dead who were in them, and they were judged, each one of them, according to what they had done" (Revelation 20:13). That liquid graveyard—where all except eight people drowned in Noah's day; in which Pharaoh and his army were drowned in Moses' day; and in which countless numbers have met their watery end over the years—that liquid graveyard will have no place in the new heaven and the new earth.

Day 5: Waters Teem with Living Creatures

As the week of creation progresses, one notices a certain pattern emerging. First God creates something or some area; later He fills it with creatures that are appropriate for it. There is a clear correspondence between the first half and the second half of the week of creation. It looks like this:

Day 1: Light and darkness	**Day 4: Sun, moon, and stars**
Day 2: Waters above and below	**Day 5: Flying and swimming creatures**
Day 3: Land and vegetation	**Day 6: Man and land animals**
Day 7: Day of rest	

Connect Genesis 1:2 with 1:20. Why is the Spirit hovering over these waters? What does He do in them?

Notice the connection between Genesis 1:2 and what happens on the fifth day of creation. The Spirit of God, who is hovering over the surface of the waters, brings forth from these waters "swarms of living creatures" (1:20). Where the Spirit of God is, there is life, and life in abundance. Jesus says, "It is the Spirit who gives life" (John 6:63). Paul echoes this in his Letter to the Romans, "The Spirit gives life" (2 Corinthians 3:6). We confess this truth of Scripture in the Nicene Creed: "I believe in the Holy Spirit, the *Lord and giver of life*" (Third Article). From the Spirit comes life—not a wheezing, staggering life, but a never-ending, strong, divine life.

This is illustrated in Genesis. Where the Spirit is hovering, when the Word of God is spoken by the Father, there is abundant life. The water is far from lifeless; it teems with living creatures.

Can you locate the Trinity in Genesis 1:2 and 1:20? If "God" is the Father and the "Spirit of God" is the Holy Spirit, then where is the Son? What does God do in verse 20? Compare this speaking with John 1:1–3.

Read John 6:63 and 2 Corinthians 3:6. What does the Spirit give? What kind of life is this?

So it is in the baptismal font. There the Spirit hovers, the Father speaks the Word of His Son, and that font is teeming with life, the very life of God. How appropriate it was therefore that the early church often compared Christians to fish, who are made alive in water and kept alive in water! So are we Christians made alive and kept alive in the water of the Spirit.

Rainy Days

Read Genesis 2:5–6. How did the Garden of Eden receive moisture?

Many commentators on Genesis have noted that until the great Flood in Noah's day, it is possible that no rain fell on the earth. Whether the Scriptures simply do not tell us that it rained before then, or whether it actually did not, is uncertain. Moses describes the "divine irrigation system" of Eden: "When no bush of the field was yet in the land and no small plant of the field had yet sprung up—for the LORD God had not caused it to rain on the land, and there was no man to work the ground, and a mist was going up from the land and was watering the whole face of the ground" (Genesis 2:5–6). The mist that rose from the ground accomplished the task that rain would later accomplish for the earth.

Write out Genesis 2:5–7 on the board or on newsprint. For every occurrence of the English word *ground* write *adamah* ("ground" in Hebrew) and for every occurrence of the English word *man* write *adam* ("man" in

Hebrew). Notice how this play on words demonstrates the intimate connection between man and the soil from which he was made.

With what is *adamah* ("ground") closely joined in 2:6? So was Adam made from dry dust or wet earth?

When studying the Bible it is often instructive to note the close correspondence between *when* certain things are described. When they are described back-to-back, they are often intended to be read together, to be understood together. Here in Genesis 2 Moses says that there was no man to cultivate the ground and that mist (not rain) would rise from the earth and water the whole surface of the ground. Immediately after this description, the author says that the Lord God formed man of dust from the ground. Notice the intimate connection between these two parts of the story: No rain upon the earth → no man to cultivate the ground → mist to rise from the earth to water. There are several wordplays in Hebrew that bring out the connection more clearly. Read these verses again, and observe how the Hebrew word for man (*adam*) sounds like the Hebrew word for ground (*adamah*). "The LORD God had not caused it to rain on the land, and there was no man [*adam*] to work the ground [*adamah*], and a mist was going up from the land and was watering the whole face of the ground [*adamah*]— then the LORD God formed the man [*adam*] of dust from the ground [*adamah*]" (Genesis 2:5b–7a). What is instructive is this: man is created from the same material just linked with water! The *adamah* from which *adam* is made is the *adamah* watered by God. Our origin is thus not only from dry dust, but from watered earth.

God is depicted as not afraid to "get His hands dirty." What does that tell us about how God works among His creatures? Through what elements in creation does God now work to give us His gifts of forgiveness, life, and salvation?

Once again we should note how God is at work.

He wants to show us from the beginning—literally!—that He is not afraid to get His hands dirty. He likes creation, indeed, He loves creation. And the things of creation are the means by which God gives us good gifts. He makes man from the wet ground. He is the God who creates man and sustains man through the stuff under man's feet, all around Him.

Read Romans 5:12–21. With whom is Jesus compared and contrasted? If we are all born from the First Adam (who had his origin in wet earth), how are we reborn in the Second Adam, Jesus Christ?

This is the way God still works in our lives. He works sacramentally, that is, He takes in hand the stuff of creation to re-create us, to remake us. And the stuff of creation He uses is water. Just as man was formed from watered ground, so man is reformed from "watered ground." In Baptism, man is washed into the body of Jesus, the man who was formed from the "virgin ground" of Mary's womb. The "ground" of Jesus' flesh is the place of our new creation. Here our sins are washed away, and we are made the children of God. The fallen children of Adam and Eve become the resurrected children of our Father who is in heaven. As a result, we are welcomed into the new Garden of Eden, the holy Christian church. Once again we are in God's holy space, where He Himself is present in our midst.

The River of Eden

Could you have pointed to the Garden of Eden on a map? In other words, was it a physical place?

Read Revelation 22:1–2 and Isaiah 11:6–9. Which elements of the Garden of Eden are both historical and real, as well as symbolic of a new and better Garden of Eden, that is, heaven itself?

Eden was a place that was physical and historical. It was not merely a place in a fictional story. It was not a mythical locale. It was a place you could have pointed to on a map. But at the same time, it

was also symbolic. It pointed beyond itself toward a greater reality that was to come in the fullness of time. It was a preview of the dwelling place of God with men, the church of our Lord Jesus Christ. Thus while its physical features were just as real and physical as any garden today, those physical features pointed beyond themselves to a greater reality of the future, a greater reality that has now come in the person of Jesus Christ. In Him we have a new and better tree of life (Genesis 2:9; Revelation 22:2); in Him the animal kingdom lives at peace with men and women (Isaiah 11:6–9); and in Him we have a new and better river that flows out of Eden (Revelation 22:1).

The number 4 is often used in the Bible to indicate all of creation. If the one river flowing out of Eden split into four rivers, what is the implication of this?

What is this river? Moses writes, "A river flowed out of Eden to water the garden, and there it divided and became four rivers" (Genesis 2:10). So, in addition to the mist that rose from the earth to water the surface of the ground, the river that flowed out of Eden served the purpose of irrigating the garden. But a single river it did not remain. Once it flowed out of Paradise it split into four rivers: the Pishon, Gihon, Tigris, and the Euphrates. That there were four of these rivers is noteworthy. The number 4 in Scripture frequently connotes the whole creation. In creation there are four winds, four corners, four directions. The biblical writer may be indicating that the life of all creation, the life embodied in water, sprang from the Garden of Eden. It was the "heart" of earth's body, the place that pumped life into the veins of the rest of creation.

Read Isaiah 2:1–4. The Hebrew verb that means "to stream" is used to describe the coming of the nations to the mountain of God. Comparing Isaiah 2 with Genesis 2, what might Isaiah be implying?

The prophet Isaiah adopts some of the imagery of Eden when he depicts the beauty and cosmological influence of the kingdom of the Messiah, including the imagery of a river. We read in Isaiah 2:1–4:

The word that Isaiah the son of Amoz saw concerning Judah and Jerusalem. It shall come to pass in the latter days that the mountain of the house of the LORD shall be established as the highest of the mountains, and shall be lifted up above the hills; and all the nations shall flow to it, and many peoples shall come, and say: "Come, let us go up to the mountain of the LORD, to the house of the God of Jacob, the He may teach us His ways and that we may walk in His paths." For out of Zion shall go the law, and the word of the LORD from Jerusalem. He shall judge between the nations, and shall decide disputes for many peoples; and they shall beat their swords into plowshares, and their spears into pruning hooks; nation shall not lift up sword against nation, neither shall they learn war anymore.

The "mountain of the house of the LORD" is Old Testament language for the church of the Messiah. It is elevated above all creation for it is the dwelling place of God with people, as in the Old Testament Mount Moriah was the place where God dwelt in Jerusalem within His temple. This mountain is the place where peace reigns, where swords become plowshares and spears become pruning hooks.

The mountain is also the place to which the nations will "flow." The Hebrew word for "nations," *goyim*, refers to all the Gentile nations, peoples from the four corners of the earth. They will figuratively "flow" up to this mountain. In the first Eden, the one river went out of the Garden and spread into four rivers and (by implication) the four corners of the world. However, in the second Eden, peoples from all over the globe will *flow into* the Paradise, where God is present to grant peace and to teach His Word. This prophecy of Isaiah is the flip side of the coin from Matthew 28:18–20. In that text Jesus sends His apostles out into all the world to make disciples of all nations. In Isaiah we have the picture rounded out for us. Indeed, the apostles "go out," but they go out precisely in order to bring in! They place people into the "river of Baptism" by which they are carried upward, by the pull of the Spirit, to Mount Eden, the paradise where God has placed His throne.

The prophet Ezekiel, like Isaiah, also uses the images of Eden, and especially the river that flows out of Paradise, to paint a picture of the salvation we have in the Messiah. In chapters 40–48 of his book Ezekiel describes his vision of the new temple that is built in "the land of Israel . . . on a very high mountain" (40:2). This whole vision is a picture of the Christian church painted in Old Testament colors. It does not describe a physical temple that will be built in the modern land of Israel. Rather, it describes the temple of Christ's church, the holy place where He resides in His grace and mercy.

In Ezekiel 40–48 the prophet describes his vision of a temple. This temple represents the kingdom of the Messiah, that is, the church. What kind of river does Ezekiel see flowing from this temple (Ezekiel 47:1–12)? Describe where it comes from, where it goes, and what it does. Compare this river with the river in Revelation 22:1–2. How are they similar?

In one part of the vision Ezekiel describes a life-giving river that flows out of the temple.

Then he brought me back to the door of the temple, and behold, water was issuing from below the threshold of the temple toward the east (for the temple faced east). The water was flowing down from below the south end of the threshold of the temple, south of the altar. Then he brought me out by way of the north gate and led me around on the outside to the outer gate that faces toward the east; and behold, the water was trickling out on the south side.

Going on eastward with a measuring line in his hand, the man measured a thousand cubits, and then led me through the water, and it was ankle-deep. Again he measured a thousand, and led me through the water, and it was knee-deep. Again he measured a thousand, and led me through the water, and it was waist-deep. Again he measured a thousand, and it was a river that I could not pass through, for the water had risen. It was deep enough to swim in, a river that could not be passed through. And he said to me, "Son of man, have you seen this?"

Then he led me back to the bank of the river. As I went back, I saw on the bank of the river very many trees on the one side and on the other. And he said to me, "This water flows toward the eastern region and goes down into the Arabah, and enters the sea; when the water flows into the sea, the water will become fresh. And wherever the river goes, every living creature that swarms will live, and there will be very many fish. For this water goes there, that the waters of the sea may become fresh; so everything will live where the river goes. Fishermen will stand beside the sea. From Engedi to Eneglaim it will be a place for the spreading of nets. Its fish will be of very many kinds, like the fish of the Great Sea. But its swamps and marshes will not become fresh; they are to be left for salt. And on the banks, on both sides of the river, there will grow all kinds of trees for food. Their leaves will not wither, nor their fruit fail, but they will bear fresh fruit every month, because the water for them flows from the sanctuary. Their fruit will be for food, and their leaves for healing." (Ezekiel 47:1–12)

What a river this is! It begins inside the temple, flowing out of the temple's side, just as water flowed from the side of the temple of Christ's body in His crucifixion (John 2:21; 19:34). As it flows down toward the Dead Sea, it gets deeper and deeper. And everywhere it goes, it gives life and it heals. Just like the river in Paradise gave life to the plants and trees of Eden, then flowed out in the four rivers to give life to all creation, so this river flows out of the very source of life itself—God—to grant life to creation.

Now compare this vision of Ezekiel with St. John's vision of the new Jerusalem. "Then the angel showed me the river of the water of life, bright as crystal, flowing from the throne of God and of the Lamb through the middle of the street of the city; also, on either side of the river, the tree of life with its twelve kinds of fruit, yielding its fruit each month. The leaves of the tree were for the healing of the nations" (Revelation 22:1–2). Here St. John fuses the two testaments together in one united picture of the new temple, the new river, the new Eden, and the new life that comes in Jesus Christ through water. The "river of the water of life" comes from the throne of God and of the Lamb. This throne is the Garden of Eden (Genesis), the mountain of the house of the Lord (Isaiah), the new temple (Ezekiel), and the crucified body of Jesus Christ (John). All of

these images of God's dwelling place are united in one composite picture. The river flows down the middle of the street of the new Jerusalem (Revelation 21:1–27). On either side of the river is the tree of life. The tree from which we once were barred by sword-bearing angels (Genesis 3:24) is now there for us to consume its fruit. It is watered by the river that proceeds from the Father and the Son, as the Holy Spirit proceeds from both. It is the Spirit's river, the river by which the Spirit grants life in its waters. The trees that grow along its banks give fruit all year round, and its leaves are for the healing of the nations. The leaves that Adam and Eve once sewed together to cover their naked bodies are now leaves that provide healing for our sin-sick souls and bodies, leaves that cover us with the healing righteousness of Jesus.

Read John 19:34. What flowed from the side of Jesus when He was crucified? How is this "river" from Jesus' side the same river that Ezekiel saw flowing from the side of the temple? (See also John 2:21.)

How do we have access to this river?

We have access to this river *already now*, for it is the river of Baptism. Baptism is the river of the water of life. It is the river that flowed from the spear-pierced side of Jesus on the cross. It is the river that is made crimson by His healing blood. Baptism carried us back into the Garden of Eden, back into God's presence. Baptism gives us access to the body and blood of Jesus in the Supper, the new tree of life. Baptism clothes us not with fig leaves, but with the body of Jesus (Galatians 3:27). People from all four corners of the world are washed in this river. The Spirit carries them on these watery waves back to where God dwells in peace, mercy, and paradise.

Conclusion: In the Beginning and in the End

"Jesus Christ is the same yesterday and today and forever" (Hebrews 13:8). He is always faithful toward His people, His church. And part of His fidelity is His consistent manner of giving us His gifts. He is not constantly changing His mind, devising some new and creative means whereby He can bless His children.

One of those consistent means is water. From the beginning, God especially singles out water as the element of creation to which He joins His Word to grant life, healing, unity, and peace. From the Garden of Eden to the new Jerusalem, there is never a drought of God's mercy, a mercy saturated with His love and reddened with the blood of His Son. All of these various uses of water point toward and culminate in the baptismal font. Here is the water that unites heaven to earth, the liquid teeming with life, the river of Eden. Here is where we fallen sons and daughters of Adam and Eve are reborn and re-created. Our sin-parched souls are flooded with His forgiving grace.

Closing Prayer

With one accord, O God, we pray,
Grant us Your Holy Spirit;
Help us in our infirmity
Through Jesus' blood and merit;
Grant us to grow in grace each day
By holy Baptism that we may
Eternal life inherit.

("All Who Believe and Are Baptized" [*LW* 225:2])

CREATION

In the Beginning . . . Everything Was Wet!

Read **Genesis 1 and 2**. Locate all the verses that mention water.

How does God interact with creation? Is He pictured as distant or close, involved or uninvolved? What does this tell us about God's relationship with creation?

Day 1: The Spirit of God and Water

Which persons of the Trinity are explicitly mentioned in the first two verses of **Genesis 1**?

Compare **Genesis 1:1–5** with **2 Peter 3:1–7**. Out of what does Peter say the earth was formed? What does that tell you about the prominence of water in the creation account?

Where is the Spirit, and what is He doing? Would it be correct to say that the Spirit is also the Creator, along with the Father? What does the Nicene Creed say about the Spirit in this regard?

Why might it be that the Spirit is described as "moving" or "fluttering"? With what bird is the Spirit later associated?

Read **Genesis 1:1–5** in light of **Matthew 3:16** and **2 Corinthians 5:17**. In what way is the Spirit present at Jesus' baptism and our Baptism? What does the Spirit create at Baptism?

Day 2: The Expanse and Separation

Read **Genesis 1:6–8**. Describe what happened on the second day of creation.

Read **Genesis 7:11–12** and **2 Peter 3:6**. Where does much of the water come from in these verses? Was the original water of creation designed by God for such punishment? Is then creation also affected by human sin? How?

Day 3: Gathering of Waters into Seas

Read **Genesis 1:9–13**. How would you summarize the work on God on the third day of creation?

What adjectives come to mind when you think of the sea: calm or troubled, safe or dangerous, peaceful or violent?

Read **Psalms 18:16; 46:2–3; 65:7; 69:1–2, 14–15; 89:9**. How did the people of Israel think of the sea? How does this compare with your picture of the sea?

Read **Matthew 8:23–27**. How is Jesus' action in the boat similar to what God did in **Genesis 1**?

Read **Revelation 20:13–21:1**. The sea is mentioned twice in these verses. Is it described in positive or negative terms? With what is the sea compared in **Revelation 20:13**? Why will there be no sea in heaven?

Day 5: Waters Teem with Living Creatures

A certain pattern emerges in **Genesis 1**. On the first three days of creation, God creates something or some area; then on the last three days of creation He fills it with creatures that are appropriate for it. Fill in the grid below according to this pattern.

Day 1:	Day 4:
Day 2:	Day 5:
Day 3:	Day 6:

Connect **Genesis 1:2** with **Genesis 1:20**. Why is the Spirit hovering over these waters? What does He do in them?

Can you locate the Trinity in **Genesis 1:2** and **1:20**? If "God" is the Father and the "Spirit of God" is the Holy Spirit, then where is the Son? What does God do in **verse 20**? Compare this speaking with **John 1:1–3**.

Read **John 6:63** and **2 Corinthians 3:6**. What does the Spirit give? What kind of life is this?

Rainy Days

Read **Genesis 2:5–6**. How did the Garden of Eden receive moisture?

With what is *adamah* ("ground") closely joined in **2:6**? So was Adam made from dry dust or wet earth?

God is depicted as not afraid to "get His hands dirty." What does that tell us about how God works among His creatures? Through what elements in creation does God now work to give us His gifts of forgiveness, life, and salvation?

Read **Romans 5:12–21**. With whom is Jesus compared and contrasted? If we are all born from the First Adam (who had his origin in wet earth), how are we reborn in the Second Adam, Jesus Christ?

The River of Eden

Could you have pointed to the Garden of Eden on a map? In other words, was it a physical place?

Read **Revelation 22:1–2** and **Isaiah 11:6–9**. What elements of the Garden of Eden are both historical and real, as well as symbolic of a new and better Garden of Eden, that is, heaven itself?

The number 4 is often used in the Bible to indicate all of creation. If the one river flowing out of Eden split into four rivers, what is the implication of this?

Read **Isaiah 2:1–4**. The Hebrew verb that means "to stream" is used to describe the coming of the nations to the mountain of God. Comparing **Isaiah 2** with **Genesis 2**, what might Isaiah be implying?

In **Ezekiel 40–48** the prophet describes his vision of a temple. This temple represents the kingdom of the Messiah, that is, the church. What kind of river does Ezekiel see flowing from this temple **(Ezekiel 47:1–12)**? Describe where it comes from, where it goes, and what it does. Compare this river with the river in **Revelation 22:1–2**. How are they similar?

Read **John 19:34**. What flowed from the side of Jesus when He was crucified? How is this "river" from Jesus' side the same river that Ezekiel saw flowing from the side of the temple? (See also **John 2:21**.)

How do we have access to this river?

NoaH aND THe FLooD

Lesson Focus

The biblical account of Noah and the Flood is one in which water is all over the place—quite literally! What are we to make of this "water story"? What message does it send about how God chooses to use water? Does it have any relation to the church today? These are the types of questions we will ask of the story in Genesis 6–9, a story full of warning and consolation.

Opening Prayer

O Lord, whose wrath burned for the evil of men, You kill and bring again to life according to Your own purpose; You brought the flood on a wicked and perverse generation yet saved faithful Noah and his family. Open Your eyes to behold in mercy Your Church that in it Your work of mercy may come to its fullness and that the ends of the earth may know Your salvation; through Jesus Christ, our Lord. Amen (Collect from the Vigil of Easter, *Lutheran Worship Agenda*, p. 82).

Not a Cute Nursery Scene

Ask participants, "In what kinds of places (outside churches) do you commonly see pictures of Noah's ark? Do you think the biblical story is a fitting theme, for instance, in a child's nursery? Why or why not?"

Imagine walking into the section of a store that has baby clothes, baby toys, baby strollers—baby everything. You name it, they've got it. In the section that has decorations for the nursery, you stop, mouth hanging open, eyes open wide. There you see colorful pictures . . . of the final judgment! There stands Christ, a double-edged sword coming out of His mouth. Demons lick their lips as they drag the souls of the damned down into the infernal pit. Other items show more joyful, but still quite serious, images. Saints clad in white sing aloud with the angels' palm branches in their hands. These scenes are painted on everything! Curtains, bottles, rattles, picture frames. No doubt, such a theme for nurseries would strike you—at best—as rather weird!

The strange thing is that, in many nurseries

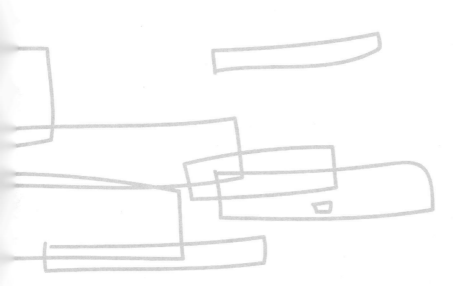

today, a biblical story that has parallels to the final judgment is used as the theme for nurseries: the story of Noah and his ark. Think about it. In this terrible Flood every single person in the world, with eight exceptions, was drowned and condemned. Only Noah, his wife, their three sons, and their daughters-in-law were spared. They alone believed in God. The rest of the world had forsaken Him, turned their backs on His Word and the promise of His Messiah (Genesis 3:15). The whole earth became a graveyard, saturated with death, above which floated the ark.

How would you summarize, in one or two sentences, the primary message of Noah and the Flood?

The story of Noah and the Flood is the real biblical story—a story of life and death, judgment and salvation, Law and Gospel. It is not a cute fairy tale in which everyone lives happily ever after.

From Bad to Worse

Skim Genesis 3–6. What are some of the high points and low points of this history?

How has humanity been affected by the coming of sin into the world?

How were the simple elements of creation affected by humanity's sin? How are fire, animals, water, the sun, and wind not only for our good, but also potentially harmful?

Reading from Genesis 3 through Genesis 6 is like reading a tragic novel that keeps getting darker and darker with each turn of the page. Though there are faint glimmers of hope and whispers of optimism scattered throughout its pages, for the most part these verses describe a world gone bad, indeed, a world going from good to bad to downright ugly. It all begins with Genesis 3, which describes the willful rebellion of the perfect husband and wife created by God. They close their ears to God's Word and open their hearts to the devil's suggestions. The end result includes the introduction of death and sin into the world. Nothing in creation remains untouched. Fire, created to serve man with warmth, now burns him. Many of the animals, made to submit to man, become wild, ravenous beasts. Water, formed to refresh man, now drowns him. Everything in the world that God said seven times was "good" and "very good" is now very bad, corrupted, spoiled by the devil and his comrades, Adam and Eve. Mankind declared war against God, and people everywhere suffer the consequences and perpetuate those consequences.

Read Genesis 3:15. What kind of promise does God make in this verse? How did this promise serve as a source of hope for Adam, Eve, and their descendants?

Read Genesis 5:28–29. What did Lamech think his newborn son would bring to the world? How does this relate to the curse in Genesis 3?

The infant son of a man named Lamech was born into this sin-filled world. For reasons we are not told, Lamech thought this boy was the promised seed (Genesis 3:15), who would reverse creation's downward spiral. He expressed this hope by giving his son the name *Noah,* which in Hebrew means "rest" or "relief." Thus Lamech said, "Out of the ground that the LORD has cursed this one [Noah] shall bring us relief from our work and from the painful toil of our hands" (Genesis 5:29). History would demonstrate that father Lamech was right—but only partially. His son, this "man of rest," would provide relief to a creation gone mad, but that relief would be partial, temporary, incomplete. Noah would not and could not eradicate the core cause of the world's problem. Indeed, Noah was part of the problem! Although a true believer, Noah was also a true sinner, just as much in need of redemption and forgiveness as the world's worst pagan. Even though Noah provided—or, rather, God *through* Noah provided—only a partial, temporary, incomplete rest, this rest still served a good and godly purpose. It was graphic preview of the true, everlasting, perfect rest that could come through a new and greater

Noah, who has a new and better ark of rescue, and who still uses water to kill but also to make alive, to drown but also to resurrect. This new and greater Noah, Jesus Christ, finishes what Noah began, finishes it perfectly in the cross, the empty tomb, and the church's baptismal font flooded with grace.

Few and Far Between

Read Genesis 6:5–8. How is Noah different from all other people? What is the basis of Noah's uniqueness, that is, what makes him different from everyone else? Was Noah good enough to meet God's standard of approval?

The story of Noah begins on a sour note. We are told what God sees when He looks down from heaven, and these words don't leave us much hope.

The LORD saw that the wickedness of man was great in the earth, and that every intention of the thoughts of his heart was only evil continually. And the LORD was sorry that He had made man on the earth, and it grieved Him to His heart. So the LORD said, "I will blot out man whom I have created from the face of the land, man and animals and creeping things and birds of the heavens, for I am sorry that I have made them." (Genesis 6:5–7)

These words are hard to swallow, but keep reading. There is light at the end of the biblical tunnel. The very next verse says, "But Noah found favor in the eyes of the LORD" (Genesis 6:8). These 10 words are a breath of fresh air. There is hope. There will be a future. There is a man who is good enough to meet God's standard of approval.

Really? Read that last sentence again. Was it because Noah was "good enough" for God, a cut above the rest, that God chose him to build the ark? Hardly. Noah was certainly "good" by human standards (he was "blameless in his generation" [Genesis 6:9]), but he was far from "good enough" for God. God requires nothing less than perfection (Leviticus 11:45). Rather, "Noah found favor in the eyes of the LORD." The Hebrew expression "to find favor in the eyes of" does not mean that a person caught someone else's eye because of high moral qualities. Rather, to find favor is to be looked upon favorably by someone else, to be seen through the eyes of grace, to be accepted regardless of personal worth or merit. Noah found favor in the eyes of the Lord because God was his gracious Father. Period. That's it. Certainly Noah had faith, but even his faith was a divine gift. Noah was chosen by God because God is who He is—the God of love and compassion.

Read Genesis 6:3 and 2 Peter 3:9. Genesis 6:3 tells us that 120 years passed from the time God decreed that He would destroy humanity until the Flood came on the earth. Why did God wait so long?

The rest of creation—with the exception of Noah's family—was outside the faith. There was still hope for them. There was still time to repent. God had given a deadline of 120 years (Genesis 6:3)—quite a long deadline, to be sure! For God is "merciful and gracious, slow to anger, and abounding in steadfast love and faithfulness" (Exodus 34:6). He is "patient toward you, not wishing that any should perish, but that all should reach repentance" (2 Peter 3:9). So the Lord gives a world of unbelievers not 40, not 80, but 120 years to confess their sin, turn to Him, and be saved.

Read 2 Peter 2:5. What does it mean that Noah was "a herald of righteousness"? What would Noah have "heralded" or proclaimed? How might Noah's message compare to a pastor's proclamation today?

The Lord did not keep silent during these 120 years. Noah was called not only to build the ark, but also to use it as a pulpit! The apostle Peter refers to Noah as "a herald of righteousness" (2 Peter 2:5), a preacher of the true faith, used by God to call an erring world to repentance. Sadly, however, his preaching fell on deaf ears and hard hearts. He gained not a single convert in 120 years of preaching! Or, if he did, they fell away before the Flood came. Still Noah preached. He did what he was given to do. He proclaimed the Word of God and left the results to his heavenly Father.

Read Matthew 24:37–39. How does Jesus use the Flood as an example in His preaching about the end of the world?

When Jesus preached about His second coming and the end of the world, He referred to Noah and his ark as an example of how people would keep going about their business, ignoring the approaching destruction. He said:

As were the days of Noah, so will be the coming of the Son of Man. For as in those days before the flood they were eating and drinking, marrying and giving in marriage, until the day when Noah entered the ark, and they were unaware until the flood came and swept them all away, so will be the coming of the Son of Man. (Matthew 24:37–39)

But those who are safe in the ark of Jesus' body, placed there by Holy Baptism, will be safe when that final flood of wrath engulfs the world. No harm will befall them. They will be with the new and better Noah, Jesus, who looked with grace and favor upon them and rescued them.

The Foolish Boat

When the Lord looked down upon creation, the world He had once pronounced "good," He saw plenty of evil. His solution (the Flood) was in part an undoing of creation. The waters that once covered the cosmos, held back by the firmament and dry land, would once again return to cover all things. It would be Genesis 1:2 all over again. But in the midst of this worldwide flood and undoing of creation, there would be another creation—the creation of a "world of salvation." This world of salvation would be a small world, to be sure, but in it would be life, a life that would continue on earth after the waters receded. The boat that Noah built was this world of salvation. In it were all those in whom the breath of life remained. And from it would come forth, by the grace of God, the seeds of a new creation.

The ark was built without sails and rudder. What does this tell us about how the movement of the ark was controlled? Who was the ark's captain?

To the eye of a sailor, the ark no doubt seemed

quite foolish. There were no sails and no rudder. It was shaped more like a huge wooden box. That indeed is what it was designed to be. It had no sails, for the Spirit of God blew the ark where He wanted it to go. It had no rudder, for God was its pilot. He alone was in control. He gave Noah instructions on the materials to use (gopher wood), the number of levels it was to have, and other particulars. But once the ark was built, the animals were loaded, and the crew of eight people were safely onboard, "the Lord shut him in" (Genesis 7:16). It was not Noah's ark, but *God's* ark. As the waters came down and the ark rose up, the Lord surrounded His boat with His angelic guards.

How were the ark and the tabernacle/temple similar? What purpose did they serve?

In the midst of the unholy death that floated all around them, the animals and Noah were enclosed by holy walls of wood. One could say that the ark was a sort of floating tabernacle or temple. Just as God dwelt in the midst of His people in the tabernacle of the desert, so He dwelt with His people in the ark. He did not leave them or forsake them. Quite the contrary! He was their captain, their guardian, the One who directed them finally to the harbor of safety, Mount Ararat.

Read Matthew 8:23–27. What kind of parallel do you see in the story of the ark and the New Testament story of Jesus in the boat with His disciples? What do both of these stories tell us about how God cares for His people?

God's gracious presence in the ark with Noah and his family is paralleled by the presence of Jesus in the boat with His disciples (Matthew 8:23–27). When the storm fell upon the lake, the waves rose, and the men thought they were soon to meet a watery end. But they were protected by the One who was in their midst. He spoke, and the winds and waves obeyed. Since, as the psalmist says, "All things are Your servants" (119:91), the waters heeded the word of their Master. All became calm. As none of Noah's family perished, though surrounded by death, so none of the disciples perished. They

were safe in God's boat.

Read Romans 6:3. How might we speak of the body of Jesus as our "ark"? How do we get into the body of Jesus?

All those who are baptized into the ark of Jesus are protected from all the winds and waves of sin, temptation, death, and hell. Though we are afloat in a world that is hostile, troubled, and constantly trying to flood our souls with doubt and unbelief, we are safe. We are at peace behind the walls of our boat. These are not walls of wood, but walls of flesh. Our ark is a body of flesh and blood, the ark born of Mary, crucified and risen. Not only is He our ark, He is our new and better temple. He is the Word made flesh who "tabernacled" among us (John 1:14). Jesus Himself tells us that His body is the temple of God, "destroyed" in His death but "rebuilt" in His resurrection (John 2:19–21). We are safe in this ark, secure in this temple. Who can harm us? No one, for no one can harm Jesus.

The Holy Octagon

How many people were in the ark?

As you read Genesis 1:1–2:3, you will notice how each day is said to have an evening and a morning. On which day, however, is there no mention of an evening and a morning?

Noah was the pastor of one of the smallest congregations ever. A grand total of eight people were in his parish! Four men and four women were inside the ark of the church. When St. Peter refers to the Flood to show how it was a preview of Baptism, he makes special mention of the number of souls on the ark: "God's patience waited in the days of Noah, while the ark was being prepared, in which a few, that is, eight persons, were brought safely through water" (1 Peter 3:20). Is there any significance to the number 8?

As a matter of fact, there is huge significance to the number 8, especially in reference to water! To begin with, we must note that 7 is the number of creation. God made the heavens and the earth in seven days (Genesis 1–2). As Genesis describes these seven days, these words are repeated as the daily refrain, "And there was evening and there was morning, the first . . . the second . . . the third day," and so forth—with the exception of the last, the seventh. Here the pattern is broken. There is no mention of the close of the seventh day. Check it out for yourself. Nowhere does Genesis say, "And there was evening and there was morning, the seventh day." This broken pattern begs the question why? Why is there no mention of the close of this day?

Read Matthew 27:57–61. The church has traditionally suggested that there is no mention of the close of the seventh day of the first creation because it was waiting to be closed by the Messiah. What did Jesus do on the very last seventh day (Sabbath Day) before His resurrection?

Compare Jesus' words on the cross "It is finished" (John 19:30) with Genesis 2:1. How are these verses similar? In what way was the Son of God resting from all the work He had done?

On what day of the week did Jesus rise from the tomb? This day has traditionally been called the eighth day because it is the day following the seven days of the first creation.

After sin entered the world, the church, yes, even the first believers in the garden, waited eagerly for the new creation. The first creation was seven days. The new creation is fulfilled in one day. The "one day" is Easter Sunday, the "eighth" day of creation. Only the coming of the Messiah, the first Creator, could once again make things new. He wrapped up the old creation as God, the Creator Himself, suffered for sin and died on Good Friday (old creation Day 6). His burial in the tomb on the Sabbath (the old creation's seventh day) was His rest. The seven days are up. The old creation is fulfilled in the work of Christ. The Messiah ushered in the new creation when He gave His entire life, including His death and burial as a payment for all

sin. The victorious new creation was complete when Christ burst forth from the dead. He is risen! He is risen indeed! The New Adam unto the new life. The victory of the new creation begins on the eighth day, Easter Sunday. The first "eighth day" was only the beginning of many "eighth days" for believers. By faith in Christ, believers are the new creation. They are the ones who are heirs of the new heaven and new earth. "Behold, I am making all things new," He says in Revelation 21:5. St. Paul affirms the same in his Letter to the Corinthians, "Therefore, if anyone is in Christ, he is a new creation. The old has passed away; behold, the new has come" (2 Corinthians 5:17)

If the eighth day is the day of our Lord's resurrection, what meaning does the number 8 have? For instance, 8 would symbolize such gifts as life and what else?

This new creation in Jesus Christ comes on the day after the old creation has come to an end, thus it is the eighth day. This eighth day of new life in Christ has no end! The sun never sets on the day of resurrection, for darkness has been put to flight. The light of Christ's resurrection shines continually. In the new Jerusalem—where the new creation is present—there is never any darkness. As St. John says, "And night will be no more" (Revelation 22:5). It is the "eternal day" in which we now live by faith and in which we will live by sight in the church triumphant.

Our Father gives us this eighth day of new life in Jesus through Baptism. This water is "included in God's command and combined with God's word" (Small Catechism), the Word that has the same power to create as the divine Word of Genesis 1.

It creates faith in our hearts; it creates our bodies anew as temples of the Holy Spirit. It creates us again not as the offspring of Adam and Eve, but as children of our heavenly Father.

Read 1 Peter 3:20–22. What does Peter say about the ark and the number of people in the ark? Peter connects the ark with which Sacrament?

Review 2 Corinthians 5:17; Romans 6:3–4. Why do you think baptismal fonts traditionally have eight sides? How is Baptism connected with resurrection and new creation?

Think again of the eight people aboard the ark. Here we have a preview of what Baptism gives and does. St. Peter links the ark with Baptism:

God's patience waited in the days of Noah, while the ark was being prepared, in which a few, that is, eight persons, were brought safely through water. Baptism, which corresponds to this, now saves you, not as a removal of dirt from the body but as an appeal to God for a good conscience, through the resurrection of Jesus Christ, who has gone into heaven and is at the right hand of God, with angels, authorities, and powers having been subjected to Him. (1 Peter 3:20–22)

There you have it, in black-and-white! Baptism "corresponds to" what happened to those eight people on the ark. They were brought safely through the waters to inhabit a world that was very much like a "new creation," though only imperfectly and temporarily. We, the baptized, are brought safely through the waters of the font. The waters drown the old Adam within us and create in us a new man, made in the image of Christ (Colossians 3:10). Through rebirth into this eighth-day creation, we join Noah and all the church in living daily and everlastingly solely by the grace of our Father.

It is no accident that most baptismal fonts have eight sides. Here stands the fountain in which we are "re-genesised," regenerated, born anew in our Lord Jesus Christ.

The Floating Zoo

How many of each kind of animal were brought aboard the ark (Genesis 7:2)? Which part of this verse is often overlooked in retelling the story of Noah's ark?

One part of Noah's story that provides the greatest attraction to many people involves the animals onboard. They may not be able to tell you how many people were onboard the ark, but they can sure tell you how many animals were—two of each, of

course! Well, not exactly. Like many popular reviews, the true biblical story of the Flood has suffered from "undertelling." Only a few features of the account described in Genesis are reported correctly.

Many types of animals came to the ark two by two, a male and a female, to perpetuate the species. But other animals came in groups of seven. Here are the exact instructions that God gave to Noah: "Take with you seven of every kind of clean animal, a male and its mate, and two of every kind of unclean animal, a male and its mate" (Genesis 7:2 NIV). So depending on the animal, sometimes they came two by two and sometimes they came seven by seven!

The distinguishing characteristic that separated the animals and thus determined how many were to be brought onboard was whether they were "clean" or "not clean." To what does this refer? If we look later into the Pentateuch, especially in Leviticus 11, we are given the answer. In Israel unclean animals were those animals that could not be touched, eaten, or used in sacrifice (for example, pigs). Of the clean animals, however, all could be touched, some were eaten, and some were reserved for sacrifice. Although the specific laws that govern which animals are clean and which are unclean were made explicit much later at Mount Sinai, evidently these rules (or some version of them) were already known and observed by God's people in Noah's day.

Read Genesis 8:20–22. How were some of the clean animals used after Noah and his family left the ark?

Why did Noah bring onboard more clean than unclean animals? The answer is quite practical: many of the clean animals would have been quickly slaughtered once the ark safely landed. If Noah had only brought two sheep along, he would have immediately brought that species to extinction when they exited the ark!

What did Noah build when they stepped onto dry land? An altar of sacrifice!

Then Noah built an altar to the LORD and took some of every clean animal and some of every clean bird and offered burnt offerings on the altar. And when the LORD smelled the pleasing aroma, the LORD said in His heart, "I will never again curse the ground because of man, for the intention of man's heart is evil from his youth. Neither will I ever again strike down every living creature as I have done. While the earth remains, seedtime and harvest, cold and heat, summer and winter, day and night, shall not cease." (Genesis 8:20–22)

The clean animals served as a liturgical sacrifice to the Lord for bringing Noah and his family safely through the Flood.

Read John 1:29; Hebrews 9:11–15. Toward what did the Old Testament sacrifices point?

Why was the smell of the burning animals a "pleasing aroma" to God? It was not because the Lord liked this smell in and of itself; it was not because God appreciated the gratitude of Noah and the others. The only reason God was pleased with this sacrifice is the only reason God was *ever pleased* with *any* sacrifice in the Old Testament: because the bodies of these animals whose blood was shed and whose corpses were consumed by the flames of the altar pointed forward to the "Lamb of God, who takes away the sin of the world!" (John 1:29). These sacrificial animals foretold of the need for the ultimate sacrifice to be offered by Jesus. The Messiah would give Himself as an "offering for sin" (Isaiah 53:10). He would be flooded with the wrath of God against our sin. His body would become like the world in Noah's day—flooded with death, permeated with uncleanness, filled to capacity with sin. Christ, who was sacrificed in our place, would take all our sins, all our uncleanness, all our death into His own body on the tree. Paul says it like this: "For our sake He [the Father] made Him [Jesus] to be sin who knew no sin, so that in Him we might become the righteousness of God" (2 Corinthians 5:21). Martin Luther referred to this as the "blessed exchange," in which Jesus exchanged our sin for His righteousness, our death for His life, our place as condemned and guilty with His place as justified and innocent. With His sacrifice the Father was well-pleased, as Isaiah says, "Yet it was the will of the LORD to crush Him" (Isaiah 53:10). One could

say it like this: Because the sacrifices that Noah and (later) all Israel offered up "smelled like" the sacrifice of Christ, being already filled with the aroma of the sacrifice to be offered by Jesus, they were pleasing to God our heavenly Father.

Cosmic Font or Graveyard?

The destructive, punitive nature of the waters of the Flood is obvious. These waters were sent by God to kill—plain and simple. There's no getting around that truth, nor should we want to. The judgment of God is always sure, always right, always truly just. We might not always understand it, but to the judgment we must say, "Amen," the word of faith.

Martin Luther's "Flood Prayer" has been used in the liturgy of Holy Baptism for the last 400 years. What kinds of connections does it make between the Flood, the ark, and Baptism?

As we read earlier, St. Peter himself places the Flood and Baptism side by side to show their resemblances (1 Peter 3:21). The Flood was a type of Baptism. But how? An excellent answer to that question is indicated in what is traditionally known as Martin Luther's "Flood Prayer," part of the liturgy sometimes prayed when a person is about to be baptized. Part of that prayer reads as follows:

O almighty God, who according to Thy righteous judgment didst condemn the unbelieving world through the flood and in Thy great mercy didst preserve believing Noah and his family . . . We pray through . . . Thy boundless mercy that Thou wilt graciously behold this (name) and bless him with true faith in his spirit so that by means of this saving flood all that has been born in him from Adam and which he himself has added thereto may be drowned in him and engulfed, and that he may be sundered from the number of the unbelieving, preserved dry and secure in the holy ark of Christendom, serve Thy name at all times fervent in spirit and joyful in hope, so that with all believers he may be made worthy to attain eternal life according to Thy promise; through Jesus Christ, our Lord. Amen. (Luther's Works 53:97)

Read Romans 6:3–6. In Noah's day the Flood produced both death and life. It was death for some and life for others. In what way is the water of Baptism both death and life?

This prayer declares the truth about Baptism that is often downplayed: Baptism not only enlivens, but it also kills. These waters carry out a divine execution—God's death penalty upon the sinner. As the prayer states, ". . . so that by means of this saving flood all that has been born in him from Adam and which he himself has added thereto may be drowned in him and engulfed." This is what St. Paul says in Romans:

Do you not know that all of us who have been baptized into Christ Jesus were baptized into His death? We were buried therefore with Him by baptism into death, in order that, just as Christ was raised from the dead by the glory of the Father, we too might walk in newness of life. For if we have been united with Him in a death like His, we shall certainly be united with Him in a resurrection like His. We know that our old self was crucified with Him in order that the body of sin might be brought to nothing, so that we would no longer be enslaved to sin. (Romans 6:3–6, emphasis added)

Paul says that Baptism kills us and buries us by uniting us to the crucifixion death of Jesus. We are crucified with Him, killed with Him, buried with Him, and raised with Him to newness of life—all by Baptism. By this water God both executes us and resurrects us. It is water of death and life.

If this flood was like Baptism, how are the two related? Is not Baptism all about life, not death, about forgiveness, not punishment? Are not the Flood and Baptism actually total opposites?

Baptism is thus like the Flood because the Flood both put to death and sustained life. The Flood put to death unbelievers, just like Baptism puts to death the old Adam, the unbelieving sinful nature in each of us. And the Flood sustained the life of the eight believers, just as Baptism grants life everlasting and sustains that life. Was the Flood therefore more like a cosmic font or cosmic graveyard? It was actually both, just as the font is for us the place of

death and burial and resurrection to a life in Jesus Christ that will never end.

The Spirit and the Dove

Read Genesis 8:6–12. Toward the end of the Flood Noah released two birds. What were these birds, and how often were they released?

One final episode in the Flood is important to note, especially in relation to the baptism of Jesus. Toward the end of Noah's many months on the ark (375 days, to be exact!), he opened the window in the ark to release a raven (Genesis 8:6–7). The raven, we are told, flew here and there until the waters dried up. Shortly afterward, Noah sent out a dove three times (Genesis 8:8–12). The first time it returned to him as it had left; the second time it returned with a freshly plucked olive leaf; the third time the dove did not return, thereby signaling that it was time for Noah and his family to say good-bye to their vessel.

What kind of message does the dove send?

This dove hovering over the surface of the waters of the Flood reminds us of the Holy Spirit, who hovered over the surface of the waters on the first day of creation (Genesis 1:2). Both the dove and the Spirit were present over waters at the genesis of something—the Spirit at the beginning of the first creation, the dove at the beginning of the post-Flood creation.

Read Matthew 3:16–17. In what other "water story" is the dove a central part of the account? How are these two "doves" similar?

Now leap forward to another creation—really, a re-creation. Leap forward to the baptism of Jesus in the Jordan River. St. Matthew tells us, "When Jesus was baptized, immediately He went up from the water, and behold, the heavens were opened to Him, and He saw the Spirit of God descending like a dove and coming to rest on Him; and behold, a voice from heaven said, 'This is My beloved Son, with whom I am well pleased' " (Matthew 3:16–17).

The Spirit of God, in the form of a dove, rested upon Jesus, for He is the Savior who brings us a new genesis. In Him we are made anew. We are rescued from the threatening perils of our sins and given citizenship in heaven. When Jesus is baptized in the waters of the Jordan, He steps into our shoes, takes our place, for He came to swallow the flood of our sins and divine wrath. Just as the dove in Noah's day was the signal that the killing waters had dried up, so the Spirit's dove on Jesus is the signal that in Him the killing waters of our iniquity will be dried up in Him. As He told John the Baptist, "Let it be so now, for thus it is fitting for us to fulfill all righteousness" (Matthew 3:15). All righteousness has been fulfilled in Jesus, for all our unrighteousness has filled Him. God holds up each of us, like bottles filled with poison, and empties them into His Son on the cross. Then, having been emptied, we are filled with the healing holiness and righteousness of Jesus. Moreover, the Spirit rests on us. We become His temple. We belong to Him.

Conclusion: The Church's Ark

St. Cyprian, one of the early church fathers, compared the church to the ark, noting that just as there was no salvation outside the ark, so there is no salvation outside the church. Cyprian was right. The church of Jesus Christ floats in a world inundated with sin and swamped in death. The only place of safety and salvation is in the boat that is built, as it were, from the wood of the cross and sealed with the blood of Jesus. Here we do not merely survive; we live in abundant grace, joy, and peace. Inside the walls of our ark is the presence of the Father, Son, and Holy Spirit.

But we must be killed to get there. We must die to be made alive. We must be flooded with the water of Baptism, drowned, then enlivened by the Spirit of Christ, breathing into our bodies and souls the very life of God. That is how we get onto and into the boat of salvation. And in that boat we shall remain until we reach the harbor of heaven above.

Closing Prayer

Sin, disturb my soul no longer:
I am baptized into Christ!
I have comfort even stronger:
Jesus' cleansing sacrifice.
Should a guilty conscience seize me
Since my Baptism did release me
In a dear forgiving flood,
Sprinkling me with Jesus' blood?

NoaH aND THe FLOOD

From Bad to Worse

Skim **Genesis 3–6**. What are some of the high points and low points of this history? How has humanity been affected by the coming of sin into the world?

How were the simple elements of creation affected by humanity's sin? How are fire, animals, water, the sun, and wind not only for our good, but also potentially harmful?

Read **Genesis 3:15**. What kind of promise does God make in this verse? How did this promise serve as a source of hope for Adam, Eve, and their descendants?

Read **Genesis 5:28–29**. What did Lamech think his newborn son would bring to the world? How does this relate to the curse in **Genesis 3**?

Few and Far Between

Read **Genesis 6:5–8**. How is Noah different from all other people? What is the basis of Noah's uniqueness, that is, what makes him different from everyone else? Was Noah good enough to meet God's standard of approval?

Genesis 6:3 tells us that 120 years passed from the time God decreed that He would destroy humanity until the Flood came on the earth. Why did God wait so long? (See **Exodus 34:6** and **2 Peter 3:9**.)

Read **2 Peter 2:5**. What does it mean that Noah was "a herald of righteousness"? What would Noah have "heralded" or proclaimed? How might Noah's message compare to a pastor's proclamation today?

Read **Matthew 24:37–39**. How does Jesus use the Flood as an example in His preaching about the end of the world?

The Foolish Boat

The ark was built without sails and rudder. What does this tell us about how the movement of the ark was controlled? Who was the ark's captain?

Besides size, how were the ark and the tabernacle/temple similar? What purpose did they serve?

Read **Matthew 8:23–27.** What kind of parallel do you see in the story of the ark and the New Testament story of Jesus in the boat with His disciples? What do both of these stories tell us about how God cares for His people?

Read **Romans 6:3.** How might we speak of the body of Jesus as our "ark"? How do we get into the body of Jesus?

The Holy Octagon

How many people were in the ark?

As you read **Genesis 1:1–2:3,** you will notice how each day is said to have an evening and a morning. On which day, however, is there no mention of an evening and a morning?

Read **Matthew 27:57–61.** The church has traditionally suggested that there is no mention of the close of the seventh day of the first creation because it was waiting to be closed by the Messiah. What did Jesus do on the very last seventh day (Sabbath Day) before His resurrection?

Compare Jesus' words on the cross "It is finished" **(John 19:30)** with **Genesis 2:1.** How are these verses similar? In what way was the Son of God resting from all the work He had done?

On what day of the week did Jesus rise from the tomb? This day has traditionally been called the eighth day because it is the day following the seven days of the first creation.

If the eighth day is the day of our Lord's resurrection, what meaning does the number 8 have? For instance, 8 would symbolize such gifts as life and what else?

Read **1 Peter 3:20–22.** What does Peter say about the ark and the number of people in the ark? Peter connects the ark with which Sacrament?

Review **2 Corinthians 5:17; Romans 6:3–4.** Why do you think baptismal fonts traditionally have eight sides? How is Baptism connected with resurrection and new creation?

may be drowned in him and engulfed, and that he may be sundered from the number of the unbelieving, preserved dry and secure in the holy ark of Christendom, serve Thy name at all times fervent in spirit and joyful in hope, so that with all believers he may be made worthy to attain eternal life according to Thy promise; through Jesus Christ, our Lord. Amen. (Luther's Works 53:97)

The Floating Zoo

How many of each kind of animal were brought aboard the ark **(Genesis 7:2)**? Which part of this verse is often overlooked in retelling the story of Noah's ark?

Read **Romans 6:3–6.** In Noah's day the Flood produced both death and life. It was death for some and life for others. In what way is the water of Baptism both death and life?

Read **Genesis 8:20–22.** How were some of the clean animals used after Noah and his family left the ark?

The Spirit and the Dove

Read **Genesis 8:6–12.** Toward the end of the Flood Noah released two birds. What were these birds, and how often were they released?

Read **John 1:29; Hebrews 9:11–15.** Toward what did the Old Testament sacrifices point?

What kind of message does the dove send?

Cosmic Font or Graveyard?

The following prayer is called Martin Luther's "Flood Prayer." It has been used in the liturgy of Holy Baptism for the last 400 years. What kinds of connections does it make between the Flood, the ark, and Baptism?

Read **Matthew 3:16–17.** In what other "water story" is the dove a central part of the account? How are these two "doves" similar?

O almighty God, who according to Thy righteous judgment didst condemn the unbelieving world through the flood and in Thy great mercy didst preserve believing Noah and his family . . . We pray through . . . Thy boundless mercy that Thou wilt graciously behold this (name) and bless him with true faith in his spirit so that by means of this saving flood all that has been born in him from Adam and which he himself has added thereto

CROSSING THE RED SEA

Lesson Focus

Like the faithless children of Israel we often find ourselves "between a rock and a hard place," suffering the ill effects of our sin. But just as God rescued the Israelites at the Red Sea, He rescues us from sin and death through the death and resurrection of His own Son, Jesus Christ.

Opening Prayer

O God, You once delivered Your people Israel from bondage under Pharaoh and led them in safety through the Red Sea, thereby giving us a picture of our Baptism. Grant that we may ever be faithful to Your baptismal promise, live in its grace, and show forth to all people Your desire that all should be made the children of Abraham; through Jesus Christ, our Lord. Amen (Collect from the Vigil of Easter, *Lutheran Worship Agenda*, p. 82).

Trapped

Military planners have to bear many things in mind when pursuing or being pursued by the enemy. They must consider methods of attack, means of escape, and whatever natural obstacles might help or hinder their efforts. Jungles are hard to advance through; deserts are difficult to cross; large bodies of water present unique challenges. Every possible scenario has to be borne in mind, lest troops get caught between a rock and a hard place, trapped in a corner with nowhere to go but the grave.

Trapped—that was the plight of the people of God in Exodus 14. When the Israelites pitched their camp at the Red Sea shortly after leaving bondage in Egypt, they stopped at a place that was militarily nothing short of foolish. They camped right beside the Red Sea, on the Egyptian shore. Mice snoozing in a cat's food dish could hardly have been more vulnerable. They soon realized this when the Egyptian army advanced against them. They were caught between bloodthirsty warriors and an Israelite-thirsty sea. They were trapped, with only two options, neither of which they would be able to survive. They could advance against the army of Egypt and be

killed by blades, or they could walk into the Red Sea and be killed by water. The end had come, or so they thought. All they could see was what they viewed with the naked eye, and their 20/20 vision spied only death. They were living by sight, not by faith.

But faithless though they were, God remained faithful. He held back the Egyptians, He parted the Red Sea, He led Israel safely through, and He destroyed their enemy. God took off the gloves for His people. He showed them that what they thought was impossible was quite possible for Him. With a snap of His fingers or, rather, a speaking of His Word, He opened up the Red Sea as easily as one swings open a door. The water they thought would be their grave turned out to be their gateway to life. The Lord showed them—and us—that He is the God of the water, the God who uses water to save, to rescue, to lead His people out of death and slavery to life and freedom.

Enslavement and Passover Freedom

Briefly review the history of Genesis 38–50. How did Jacob and his sons end up in Egypt? Was this the land on which they were permanently to settle?

Read Exodus 1:1–7. What kind of blessings did God give the Israelites while they were in Egypt?

In order to understand the plight of the Israelites at the Red Sea, it is necessary first to remember the situation from which they had just been rescued. The last few chapters of Genesis record how Joseph—who had become Pharaoh's right-hand man—relocated his father, Jacob (a.k.a. Israel), and his 11 brothers from Canaan to Egypt. Pharaoh gave them Goshen, a fertile region of land in Egypt, as their homeland. They settled there with their families and herds. They sank deep roots in Egypt. Life was good. God blessed them on foreign soil. But this was not to last forever.

Read Exodus 1:8–22. What changed the situa-

tion of the Israelites? What were the plans devised by Pharaoh that caused such suffering among the people of Israel?

The opening verses of the sequel to Genesis, the Book of Exodus, describe how "there arose a new king over Egypt, who did not know Joseph" (Exodus 1:8). But what he *did* know (or, at least, thought he knew) was that the multitude of Israelites living on Egyptian soil presented a threat to his country's national security. Thus, he and his successors hatched several inhumane plans to try to strengthen their grip on Israel, "lest they multiply, and, if war breaks out, they join our enemies and fight against us and escape from the land" (Exodus 1:10). These two plans were the enslavement of the Israelites (and with that, forced labor) and the murder of the male infants of the Israelites.

Briefly review the history of Exodus 2–12 from the chart on the participant page. Whom did the Lord send to rescue the people of Israel (Exodus 3)? What did God do to the Egyptians when Pharaoh refused to let the Israelites go (Exodus 7–11)? How did the Israelites finally get out of Egypt (Exodus 12)?

In order to rescue His oppressed people, the Lord sent Moses. He and his brother, Aaron, were God's human instruments by which He brought nine successive plagues upon Pharaoh and the Egyptians. Still the king would not let the Israelites go. The tenth plague, however, finally broke the king's strong grip. In this plague the Lord sent His destroying angel throughout Egypt to slay all the firstborn males of Egypt. God's people, however, were protected from this angel by the blood of a sacrificial lamb, which had been painted on the doorposts and lintels of their homes. Safe inside their houses, the Israelites consumed the meat of the lamb, the Passover sacrifice, while the Egyptians all around them were consumed by death. The next morning, while the Israelites left the country that had enslaved them, the Egyptians were digging graves for their sons.

Read Exodus 14:1–9. Where did the Israelites camp after they left Egypt? How was this part
of God's plan? Who had a "change of heart" after the Israelites left?

The story was far from over, however. Not long afterward, Pharaoh had a change of heart—one more manifestation of his hard heart! He gathered his chariots and soldiers and took off in hot pursuit of his former slaves. When he discovered they were camped beside the Red Sea, with nowhere to go, he must have thought, Now, I will get my revenge!

Little did Pharaoh know that he was heading straight into a trap. The Lord set the bait, and Pharaoh eagerly grabbed it.

During the course of the 10 plagues, the Scriptures say several times that Pharaoh hardened his own heart (Exodus 7:14, 22; 8:15, 19, 32). Not until after the sixth plague does it say that "the Lord hardened the heart of Pharaoh" (Exodus 9:12). So, who is responsible for the hardness of Pharaoh's heart—God or Pharaoh?

What kind of comparisons would you make between Pharaoh and Satan? What is their attitude toward God? How do they treat the people of God?

Read Romans 6:6; Ephesians 4:22; and Colossians 3:9. What does St. Paul mean by the "old self" in us? How is the "old self" in each of us like Pharaoh?

This king of Egypt, the leader of the nation that had enslaved Israel, is not unlike another leader who has enslaved countless multitudes over the centuries. He is devious and ruthless, drunk with hatred yet sober with vigilance, always keeping his eyes peeled for an opportunity to tighten the shackles that bind his slaves or capture any who have escaped. He is the archenemy of truth, freedom, justice, love, and goodness. His heart is so hard that it makes flint seem like cotton. And—worst of all—this king has an accomplice, an "inside man" who works with him to keep people enslaved or trick them back into the king's cage. Who is this king and his accomplice? The king of slavery is Satan, and his accomplice is the sinful nature that dwells within each of us. He rules over the Egyptian land called sin, and unbelief is his chain.

The question is this: How is this king of slavery defeated and his shackles broken? And, what's more, how is the power of his accomplice within us—the "old self" as Paul calls him (Romans 6:6; Ephesians 4:22; Colossians 3:9)—destroyed? As we will see, both of them are destroyed through a most unlikely means—water.

Caught between Death and Death— Right Where God Wants Them!

Read Exodus 14:10–12. When the Israelites looked up to see the Egyptians heading toward them, how did they react? What did their reaction reveal about their faith? How does Psalm 106:6–7 describe the people's reaction?

If you are familiar with the stories about Israel in the wilderness, you are aware of the obvious fact that—to put it mildly—patience in the midst of suffering was not a strong point. When the Israelites exited Egypt as free men, women, and children, no doubt they were full of joy and hope. The future was bright. Everything looked good. Ahead of them lay a life in the Promised Land, a land flowing with milk and honey.

But the joy soon turned to dismay. The Israelites lifted up their eyes to spy the Egyptian chariots heading toward them. They began to whimper like three-year-olds to Moses: "Is it because there are no graves in Egypt that you have taken us away to die in the wilderness? What have you done to us in bringing us out of Egypt? Is not this what we said to you in Egypt, 'Leave us alone that we may serve the Egyptians'? For it would have been better for us to serve the Egyptians than to die in the wilderness" (Exodus 14:11–12). They were looking at their situation with the naked eye, not an eye clothed with the Word of God, not eyes that see what God sees. Indeed, what they needed to do was to "pluck out their eyeballs and stick them in their ears," that is, they needed to see through their ears, to view their

situation in light of what God had promised them, not what stared them in the face. But, alas, it was not to be.

What is faith, according to Hebrews 11:1? How does faith relate to sight? How does faith relate to the Word of God?

Why is it so difficult to live by faith and not by sight? Discuss some ways in which we are exactly like the Israelites. What have you faced in your own life that reveals a lack of faith or a weak faith?

How could the Israelites be so faithless? Ask yourself. What is painfully true is that we are no different then they. We, too, have heard the promises of God—the promises of His Word, which He has always kept, never broken. Yet when we see no possibility of escape when trapped in greed, lust, addiction—you name it—all we see is the Red Sea on one side of us and the Egyptians on the other. We see no way of escape for we don't "see through our ears." We are all too often like Peter, who was called out of the boat by Jesus and began to walk on the water toward his Lord. However, "When [Peter] saw the wind, he was afraid, and beginning to sink he cried out, 'Lord, save me.' Jesus immediately reached out His hand and took hold of him, saying to him, 'O you of little faith, why did you doubt?' " (Matthew 14:30–31). Yes, we are just as much in need of repentance, and just as much in need of increased faith, as were the whimpering Israelites and the sinking disciple.

The truth is that God *purposefully* led Israel to the place of her entrapment, and the Lord Jesus *purposefully* called Peter out of the boat onto the storm-tossed sea, precisely in order to show them that He is the God who works the possible in the face of the seemingly impossible. "With God all things are possible," Jesus affirms (Matthew 19:26). All things! "By faith we understand that the universe was created by the word of God, so that what is seen was not made out of things that are visible" (Hebrews 11:3). And this same good and gracious God, who made all things out of nothing, solely by His Word, is the same good and gracious God who brought a son out of Sarah's 90-year-old womb (Genesis 21); who brought Jonah out of the fish's belly (Jonah 2); and who brought the crucified and dead Messiah out of the tomb of death to a life that will never end (Matthew 28). He who specializes in making something out of nothing will always stick by His promises. This good and gracious God, our heavenly Father, would also bring life out of death and freedom out of slavery for the Israelites. He would unlock the gate of the sea, swing open the door, and hold Israel's hand as they walked on dry ground. Like a crying baby emerging from the birth canal, so this newborn nation would go through the canal of the sea and emerge on the other side, born anew by the creative power of God.

What does St. Paul say about weakness and strength in 2 Corinthians 12:7–10? How were the Israelites "made weak" at the Red Sea? How does God make you weak that you may be strong?

What is often best for us prideful, self-reliant sinners is to be caught like the Israelites between death and death, between our own Red Sea and our own Egyptian foes. For it is there—and only there—that we drop all our pretenses about being in control of our lives and face up to the fact that if God were to withdraw His gracious hand from us for one instant, we would fall flat on our face. When we are trapped, with no means of escape visible to the naked eye, then God begins to clothe our eyes with faith in His Word of promise and protection. So it was for Israel, so it was for Peter, so it is for us. Our Father promises never to leave us, never to forsake us, but always to deliver us from evil. His Word never lies. It never betrays or misleads you. It always comes through for it is the Word of your Savior.

Walking between Walls of Waters

When the Israelites accused Moses (and, in reality, God Himself) of leading them out of Egypt to execute them in the wilderness, Moses responded by calling the people to faith in the Lord of salvation.

He said, "Fear not, stand firm, and see the salvation of the LORD, which He will work for you today. For the Egyptians whom you see today, you shall never see again. The LORD will fight for you, and you have only to be silent" (Exodus 14:13–14). In other words, "Quit pouring out your grumbling words of unbelief and watch while the LORD pours out His salvation for you!" Moses affirms, "The LORD will fight for you."

We often say, "When you want a job done right, do it yourself." So it is with God. He works our salvation, our deliverance, all by Himself. No assistance is expected or required. He doesn't need us to supplement His work, to smooth out the rough edges, to try to "pretty it up" with our own works. He is perfectly capable of perfectly working our salvation. The Lord will fight for you. And He will win, every time. So He did at the Red Sea and on the crimson cross. He did it all, all for you, and He still does.

Read Exodus 14:15–25. How did God part the waters of the Red Sea? What parts of creation did God use as His "tools" to accomplish this miracle? Discuss what this tells us about the way God works salvation for His people. What kinds of physical things does God use today to give salvation to His people? What does He use in Baptism and in the Lord's Supper?

Even though God does it all, He doesn't do it without certain means. Mark this well. Brand it on your mind and heart. This is part of the ABCs of how God works in this world. Amazingly, many people never even get this alphabet down. They stumble over the ABCs. The Lord is not a heavenly wizard who points a magic wand toward the earth and zaps it with saving energy. Far from it. He is the God who works through people, through things, through events that are part of creation in order to save His created people. Although He could simply have zapped Egypt and Pharaoh, He does not. He works through created means. He calls a man, Moses, and sends him to rescue His people. He puts in his hand a wooden staff that is so connected with the Word of God that the staff works what God's Word says. He protects His people from death by the blood of a lamb. Yes, He alone saves, He alone protects, He alone sustains His church, but He always does so through His own chosen means of creation.

When Israel was trapped at the Red Sea and Moses promised them that God would fight for them while they stood by silently, observe how God did so through the means He had placed at His disposal. He told Moses, "Lift up your staff, and stretch out your hand over the sea and divide it, that the people of Israel may go through the sea on dry ground. . . . Then Moses stretched out his hand over the sea, and the LORD drove the sea back by a strong east wind all night and made the sea dry land, and the waters were divided. And the people of Israel went into the midst of the sea on dry ground, the waters being a wall to them on their right hand and on their left" (Exodus 14:16, 21–22). Through the staff of Moses in his uplifted hand and through a strong east wind—through wood and wind—God worked deliverance. As awesome as the parting of the waters was, the instruments used to do it were not very awesome. They had no razzle-dazzle. They were quite ordinary, down-to-earth, simple. But that is how God worked this rescue of His people.

And that is how God has worked, and still works, your rescue as well. As God sent the man Moses, so God sent His Son to become a man. As we confess in the Nicene Creed: "who for us men and for our salvation came down from heaven and was incarnate [literally, 'enfleshed'] by the Holy Spirit of the virgin Mary *and was made man*." This God-man Jesus Christ was the new and better Moses, who came to work a new and better salvation. Moreover, just as God protected His people from death by the blood of a creature—a lamb at Passover—so He protects His people from everlasting death by the blood of another creature (but a creature who is simultaneously the Creator!)—Jesus Christ, the Lamb of God whose blood is "painted" on us. In the exodus, God joined His Word to the simple wooden staff of Moses. Even so He has joined His Word to the simple stuff of creation: the bread and wine of the Lord's Supper, the body and blood of the divine Lamb. And, most obvious of all in Exodus 14, just as Israel's rescue was through

water, so our rescue has been through water as well. We pass through the Red Sea of the baptismal font, rescued from slavery and death.

How does St. Paul interpret the crossing of the Red Sea in 1 Corinthians 10:1–4? How does he compare this crossing to Baptism? How are they similar? What does it mean that they were baptized into Moses? How does this relate to what Paul says in Galatians 3:27? Who was in the pillar of cloud (see Exodus 13:21)? Who else was intimately connected with the cloud (see Exodus 14:19–20)? How might this help to explain what Paul means by being "baptized into Moses in the cloud and in the sea" (1 Corinthians 10:2)?

St. Paul explicitly links Holy Baptism to Israel's crossing of the Red Sea in his Letter to the Christians in Corinth. He says, "I want you to know, brothers, that our fathers were all under the cloud, and all passed through the sea, and all were baptized into Moses in the cloud and in the sea, and all ate the same spiritual food, and all drank the same spiritual drink. For they drank from the spiritual Rock that followed them, and the Rock was Christ" (1 Corinthians 10:1–4). The apostle is speaking by way of comparison. He says that the Israelites were "baptized into Moses"; that is, they were intimately bound to the man who was their "savior," who has led them out of Egypt through water. In a much more intimate way, we are baptized into the very body of Jesus so that His flesh and blood now cover us as the holy clothing. As Paul says elsewhere, "For all of you who were baptized into Christ have clothed yourselves with Christ" (Galatians 3:27 NIV). As vestments covered the priests of the Old Testament, allowing them to stand in the holy place of the temple, so in Baptism we are clothed with the vestments of the body and blood of Jesus, our High Priest (Hebrews 8:1), so that we can stand in God's presence, even in the holy places (Hebrews 10:19–22).

Paul says the Israelites were "baptized into Moses in the cloud and in the sea" (1 Corinthians 10:2). What does he mean by "in the cloud and in the sea"? Who was in the cloud? Exodus 13:21 tells us that "the LORD went before them by day in a pillar of cloud to lead them along the way, and by night in a pillar of fire to give them light." When the Egyptians were about to attack Israel at the Red Sea, we are told that "the angel of God who was going before the host of Israel moved and went behind them, and the pillar of cloud moved from before them and stood behind them, coming between the host of Egypt and the host of Israel" (14:19–20). So who was in the cloud? "The LORD" ("Yahweh" in Hebrew) and "the angel of God." In the Old Testament, "angel of God" is very often the form in which the Son of God appears. Although He was not and is not an angel, He temporarily assumed the form of angel to appear to His people (e.g., Exodus 3:1–6). It is, therefore, none other than the Son of God Himself who is in the cloud. St. Paul is saying to the Corinthians, "Israel was baptized into Moses in that cloud in which the Son of God was present. They were baptized in the water of the sea that Jesus had split open for them to pass through."

Read Exodus 14:13–14. How did Moses respond to the Israelites? Moses spoke these words to the Israelites, who needed to be saved from physical enemies. How do the words of Paul in Ephesians 2:8–9 echo Exodus 14:13–14? Who is doing what and who is receiving what in each of these texts?

What do you see, then, when you hold up these two pictures side by side: the picture of the people of God walking on dry ground through the Red Sea and the picture of you having water poured on you at the font? You see, as it were, a family resemblance. There is the "Red-Sea-father" and the "baptismal-font-son." Though one is older than the other, there are similarities that cannot be missed. Jesus Christ, who is "the same yesterday and today and forever," continues to use water today in the church as He used it 3,400 years ago at the border of Egypt. Some things never change! And thanks be to God that they do not. For this water is "divine water," as Martin Luther once called it (Large Catechism), for through it comes salvation for us

and for all the people of God.

Egyptians Dead on the Seashore

Read Exodus 14:24–25. How did the Lord fight for His people as He promised, through Moses, that He would?

If your ears are tuned into the music of this story of the Red Sea, you cannot help but hear echoes of the story of the Flood in Noah's day. The echoes are many, but one resounds louder than most: this water was not only a means of rescue for God's people, but also the means of destruction for unbelievers. The same type of death that the whole world—minus eight people—experienced in the Flood was the type of death that the Egyptians faced. Both drowned in the water that saved God's church.

After the Israelites traveled between the two walls of water to the safety beyond Egypt, their enemies raced after them. Blind with fury, they saw only their chance to satisfy their lust for revenge. They were like a starving fish that sees a fat worm floating in the water—easy prey except the worm conceals a barbed hook. Pharaoh had so hardened his heart by this time that he did not see the danger. All he saw was the worm. Indeed, Pharaoh had made his heart so hard for so long that the Lord began to punish him by hardening it even more (Exodus 14:8).

When did the Egyptians realize who their real enemy was (see Exodus 14:25)? What does this confession tell you about their knowledge of God? Were they sinning in ignorance or in full knowledge?

When Israel was exiting one end of the sea, the Egyptians were entering the other end. "And in the morning watch the LORD in the pillar of fire and of cloud looked down on the Egyptian forces and threw the Egyptian forces into a panic, clogging their chariot wheels so that they drove heavily. And the Egyptians said, 'Let us flee from before Israel, for the LORD fights for them against the Egyptians' " (Exodus 14:24–25). The Egyptians realized too late that they had swallowed the bait—hook, line, and sinker. There was nowhere to go. As on the Last Day, when even unbelievers will be forced to bow the knee and acknowledge to their everlasting shame that "Jesus Christ is Lord" (Philippians 2:11), so these Egyptians—on their own last day—had to confess in shame and defeat that the Lord was fighting for His church. But their confession was also their judgment, for they expressed the truth that they were fighting against the true God. They had spent their whole lives bowing down to fake gods, the many gods and goddesses that littered the landscape of Egypt. And even when the true God, Yahweh, had made it so clear in the 10 plagues that He alone was the true God of heaven and earth, still they refused to believe. Now they were reaping the poisonous fruit of their idolatry.

Egyptian legend said that when people died, they crossed the Red Sea to the life beyond. But this false legend was now laughing mockingly in their face. For it was their enemy who had crossed the sea. They, however, were trapped. Walls of water cascaded down upon them. Their watery coffin was nailed shut with blows from a divine hammer. Exodus tells of their end:

> Then the LORD said to Moses, 'Stretch out your hand over the sea, that the water may come back upon the Egyptians, upon their chariots, and upon their horsemen.' So Moses stretched out his hand over the sea, and the sea returned to its normal course when the morning appeared. And as the Egyptians fled into it, the LORD threw the Egyptians into the midst of the sea. The waters returned and covered the chariots and the horsemen; of all the host of Pharaoh that had followed them into the sea, not one of them remained. But the people of Israel walked on dry ground through the sea, the waters being a wall to them on their right hand and on their left. Thus the LORD saved Israel that day from the hand of the Egyptians, and Israel saw the Egyptians dead on the seashore. (Exodus 14:26–30)

"Egyptians dead on the seashore"—those words say it all, don't they? The picture they paint is not pretty, but neither is sin. Sin is ugly, deadly, and painful, but it has its ways of charming people. And those who give heed to its flirtatious ways, and refuse to repent, will face an ugly end.

Read Exodus 14:26–30. How did the Lord use the same water in two ways: one way for His people and the other way for the Egyptians? If Egypt is like the sinful nature in each of us, discuss how the baptismal font is like a miniature of the Red Sea.

For those who are baptized, the ugly end has already been faced and overcome. You were born with gallons of Egyptian blood coursing through your veins. Pharaoh of hell has a close friend, a partner-in-crime, who dwells in each of us. He is the "old man," or the "old Adam" as Luther called him. He cannot be reformed; he cannot be made better; he cannot be merely controlled or tamed. There is only one way to deal with him: by killing him.

And that's precisely what God has done for each of the baptized. He first killed us. He held the head of the old Adam under the waters of the Red Sea font. He was executed by divine edict. The words "I baptize you in the name of the Father and of the Son and of the Holy Spirit" say to the Egyptian in each of us: "Look up, old Adam, and see the walls of water that are falling upon you. You must die. And die you will." Along the shores of every baptismal font float the drowned bodies of old Adams.

But that is not the end. God first kills us that He might do His proper work: make us alive. He executes to resurrect. We are raised to new life in Christ. We are baptized into the body of the new and better Moses. We begin our journey toward the promised land of heaven above. We have become part of the new Israel, the church of our Lord Jesus Christ.

Conclusion

The Red Sea is colorfully and also perfectly named—at least from a biblical point of view. After reading Exodus, one cannot help but think of the crimson color of the Egyptian blood that mixed with the water of the sea called Red. But from the perspective of Baptism and the Red Sea's connection with that saving Sacrament, the name of the sea takes on even greater ramifications. For mixed with the water of the font is, so to speak, the blood of Jesus. His blood gives the water the power to kill the old man and raise to newness of life the new man. In the red font we leave Egypt behind and journey toward the heavenly fatherland. And we are still dripping wet with that water of life when we reach our home above.

Closing Prayer

All that the mortal eye beholds
Is water as we pour it.
Before the eye of faith unfolds
The pow'r of Jesus' merit.
For here it sees the crimson flood
To all our ills bring healing;
The wonders of His precious blood
The love of God revealing,
Assuring His own pardon.

("To Jordan Came the Christ, Our Lord" [LW 223:7])

CROSSING THE RED SEA

Enslavement and Passover Freedom

Briefly review the history of **Genesis 38–50.** How did Jacob and his sons end up in Egypt? Was this the land on which they were permanently to settle?

Read **Exodus 1:1–7.** What kind of blessings did God give the Israelites while they were in Egypt?

Briefly review the history of Exodus 2–12 from the chart below.

Moses hidden in a basket among the reeds, found and adopted by Pharaoh's daughter.	God gives Moses powerful signs to perform before Pharaoh. God empowers Moses' brother, Aaron, to speak for Him.	Plagues upon Egypt
Moses kills an Egyptian and flees to Midian.	Moses and Aaron return to Egypt.	Water turned to blood Frogs Gnats Flies Livestock die Boils on man and animals Hail Locusts Darkness
Moses marries Jethro's daughter Zipporah and works tending the flocks.	Pharaoh increases the Israelites' workload, but they still prosper.	Passover celebrated
Moses is called by God through the burning bush.	Moses and Aaron go to Pharaoh to demand the release of the Israelites.	Final plague— death of the firstborn

Read **Exodus 1:8–22**. What changed the situation of the Israelites? What were the plans devised by Pharaoh that caused such suffering among the people of Israel?

Read **Romans 6:6; Ephesians 4:22;** and **Colossians 3:9**. What does St. Paul mean by the "old self" in us? How is the "old self" in each of us like Pharaoh?

Skim **Exodus 2–12**. Whom did the Lord send to rescue the people of Israel? What did God do to the Egyptians when Pharaoh refused to let the Israelites go? How did the Israelites finally get out of Egypt?

Caught between Death and Death—Right Where God Wants Them!

Read **Exodus 14:10–12**. When the Israelites looked up to see the Egyptians heading toward them, how did they react? What did their reaction reveal about their faith? How does **Psalm 106:6–7** describe the people's reaction?

Read **Exodus 14:1–9**. Where did the Israelites camp after they left Egypt? How was this part of God's plan? Who had a "change of heart" after the Israelites left?

What is faith, according to **Hebrews 11:1**? How does faith relate to sight? How does faith relate to the Word of God?

During the course of the 10 plagues, the Scriptures say several times that Pharaoh hardened his own heart (**Exodus 7:14, 22; 8:15, 19, 32**). Not until after the sixth plague does it say that "the LORD hardened the heart of Pharaoh" (**Exodus 9:12**). So who is responsible for the hardness of Pharaoh's heart—God or Pharaoh?

Why is it so difficult to live by faith and not by sight? Discuss some ways in which we are exactly like the Israelites. What have you faced in your own life that reveals a lack of faith or a weak faith?

What does St. Paul say about weakness and strength in **2 Corinthians 12:7–10**? How were the Israelites "made weak" at the Red Sea? How does God make you weak that you may be strong?

What kind of comparisons would you make between Pharaoh and Satan? What is their attitude toward God? How do they treat the people of God?

Walking between Walls of Waters

Read **Exodus 14:15–25**. How did God part the waters of the Red Sea? What parts of creation did God use as His "tools" to accomplish this miracle? Discuss what this tells us about the way God works salvation for His people. What kinds of physical things does God use today to give salvation to His people? What does He use in Baptism and in the Lord's Supper?

How does St. Paul interpret the crossing of the Red Sea in **1 Corinthians 10:1–4**? How does he compare this crossing to Baptism? How are they similar? What does it mean that they were baptized into Moses? How does this relate to what Paul says in **Galatians 3:27**? Who was in the pillar of cloud (see **Exodus 13:21**)? Who else was intimately connected with the cloud (see **Exodus 14:19–20**)? How might this help to explain what Paul means by being "baptized into Moses in the cloud and in the sea" (**1 Corinthians 10:2**)?

Read **Exodus 14:13–14**. How did Moses respond to the Israelites? Moses spoke these words to the Israelites, who needed to be saved from physical enemies. How do the words of Paul in **Ephesians 2:8–9** echo **Exodus 14:13–14**? Who is doing what and who is receiving what in each of these texts?

Egyptians Dead on the Seashore

Read **Exodus 14:24–25**. How did the Lord fight for His people as He promised, through Moses, that He would?

When did the Egyptians realize who their real enemy was (see **Exodus 14:25**)? What does this confession tell you about their knowledge of God? Were they sinning in ignorance or in full knowledge?

Review **Exodus 14:26–30**. How did the Lord use the same water in two ways: one way for His people and the other way for the Egyptians? If Egypt is like the sinful nature in each of us, discuss how the baptismal font is like a miniature of the Red Sea.

4

NaaMaN's "BaPTiSM" iN THe JORDaN

Lesson Focus

Since the beginning of time we have sought solutions to the problems that plague humankind, especially the problem of sin in our lives. Like Naaman, we may find it hard to believe that the solution to sin could be as simple as water combined with the powerful Word of God. In this session we will explore the grace of God poured upon Naaman in the Jordan and us through the Word and Sacraments.

Opening Prayer

Lord God, heavenly Father, who graciously healed Your servant Naaman in the waters of the Jordan River, thereby prefiguring the healing waters of Holy Baptism, grant unto us who have been baptized Your Holy Spirit, that we may ever live in the grace of eternal healing; through Jesus Christ, our Lord. Amen.

Too Simple

Ask participants, "What are some of the typical responses people have to complex problems? Is the solution usually complex also or simple?"

We are usually hesitant to accept simple solutions to complex problems. They sound too easy. When we get ourselves entangled in some mess, the last thing we want to hear is, "The only thing you need to do is . . ." Our immediate reaction may include something such as, "Oh, if it were only that simple!" When husbands and wives have marital problems, when people get entangled in various addictions, when medical problems multiply, when all sorts of chains are wrapped tightly around our lives, we think that getting out of the mess we're in will take 10 or 50 or 100 steps that gradually lead to self-improvement and healing. Indeed, sometimes it works out that way. Often the true solution is staring us in the face. But when the solution seems so effortless and uncomplicated, we may think it is too easy to be true. Instead we opt for the complicated,

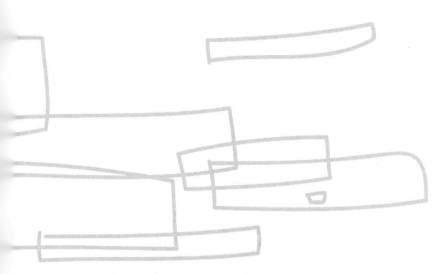

the involved, the multifaceted approach.

What is a common response to the complex problem of sin? Pinpoint various ways in which people try to "help God" by using their own strength, wisdom, willpower, and so forth to escape from sin.

The biggest problem of all is when we approach matters of sin and salvation with a "too easy to be true" kind of attitude. To be sure, our lives are often very complicated by sin. Oh, what tangled webs we weave! This vice leads to that vice, which then leads to another vice, and before you know it, our lives resemble one of those pictures of kittens all tangled up in the ball of yarn they've been playing with. But in our case, the picture is anything but cute. It's horribly ugly. We're wrapped up in lust, in greed, in hatred, in jealousy; every limb of our soul is enmeshed in these cords of iniquity. The harder we struggle against them, the tighter their hold becomes. Then along comes someone who says to us, "Repent and believe the Good News that Christ has paid for your sins." Our response to that solu-

tion is often, "Oh, sure! If only it were that simple. If only God called me to confess and believe. But it just can't be that easy."

But it really is! The Good News of salvation in Jesus is very uncomplicated, very straightforward. That, however, is the problem for sinners. For if Jesus *has done* all the work of earning our salvation, and if Jesus *will do* all the work in putting salvation into us, and if Jesus promises *to do* all the work in keeping us in that salvation, what is there left for us to do? Nothing! And there's the rub. We want to be involved. We want to do our part. The last thing we want is to be completely dependent upon another, especially another who makes the solution to our problems seem so simple. But that is the kind of God we have: a God with simple, down-to-earth solutions to our problems. And these simple, down-to-earth solutions truly do what they say and give what they promise.

Naaman—the Doubting Leper

The Syrian military officer Naaman is somewhat

the Old Testament equivalent of doubting Thomas (John 20:24–29). Just as Thomas refused to believe that the Lord Jesus had risen from the dead unless he saw in His hands the marks of the nails, placed his finger into the marks of the nails, and placed his hand into Jesus' side, so Naaman refused to believe that God would be faithful to His Word. Naaman was looking for tangible proof that God would do what He had promised. Although he had the clear Word of God from the mouth of the prophet, he wanted more, something more fantastic, something he could wrap his mind around. God's solution was far too simple for Naaman's problem.

As we will see, Naaman's story is our story. Indeed, Naaman's story is the story of every sinner. We all have a "leprosy" very much like the leprosy that attached itself to the skin of this Syrian officer. Our ailment is serious and not going away, no matter how much we try to rid ourselves of it, no matter how many complicated and extravagant solutions we devise on our own. This "leprosy" is stuck to us, embedded into the flesh of our heart and soul.

But there is a true and lasting solution. For Naaman that solution was found in the water of the Jordan River. For us that solution is found in the water of the baptismal Jordan. But the solution is indeed simple—too simple to believe, it often seems. But as it was for Naaman, so it is for us. The Lord who works through simple means to give us uncomplicated solutions is calling us to faith in His Word. It is that Word of life, flooded with grace, that gives the simple solution its saving power.

Naaman's Problem

Read 2 Kings 5:1–5. What kind of man was Naaman? Was he an Israelite? What was his nationality? What kind of relationship did the Israelites usually have with those outside their own nation?

What might Naaman's life have been like? Where would he likely have been on the social "totem pole"? At the top or bottom? What was his vocation? Does he seem to have a weak or a strong personality?

Naaman was not your typical Bible character. What especially set him apart was his nationality: he was not an Israelite. In fact, he was a leader in the armed forces of a nation that often warred against Israel! He was "commander of the army of the king of Syria . . . a great man with his master and in high favor, because by him the LORD had given victory to Syria. He was a mighty man of valor" (2 Kings 5:1). In other words, Naaman had lots of things going for him. He had power, fame, and direct access to a powerful king. No doubt, his bank account was stuffed with plenty of Syrian cash. Life was good . . . well, seemingly good.

What was Naaman's problem? How might this problem have "handicapped" Naaman socially, politically, and militarily?

Naaman's health problem may not have been—strictly speaking—what we call "leprosy" (the Hebrew word used is a general word for many types of skin disease). Whatever it was, it was certainly serious. Suppose, however, that it was leprosy. Look up the word *leprosy* in a dictionary or encyclopedia. What are the characteristics of this skin disease? What does it do to the body?

Naaman had a problem that cast a shadow over all his worldly fame, power, and wealth. At the end of the description quoted earlier, we read, "[Naaman] was a mighty man of valor, *but* he was a leper" (2 Kings 5:1, emphasis added). That "but" rendered sour all the sweet things Naaman had in life. This mighty man was afflicted with some sort of serious skin disease. It very well may have been the horrific medical disease that we call leprosy. The Hebrew word commonly translated as "leprosy" in English versions of the Bible is actually a much more general term for skin disease. Included under it would certainly be leprosy, but also any number of sicknesses that manifest themselves in the skin of the body. (For the sake of clarity and simplicity, in this study we'll assume it was leprosy.) But whether it was, strictly speaking, leprosy or some other sort of skin ailment, the results were serious. Naaman's problem was not going away. It could very well have been progressively worsening. It had embedded itself into Naaman's body, branding him for all the world to see. It was a brand that Naaman was willing to do anything to get rid of . . . well, almost anything.

Discuss how Naaman's physical sickness is similar to our spiritual sickness—sin. How are they similar? What effects do they have on the body and soul?

Read Psalm 51:5. Do we become sinners, or are we conceived as sinners? Are adults and infants, therefore, sinners? What does this say about the need for the Baptism of people of all ages, including children?

Naaman the leper was a walking picture of the spiritual disease that every person has from the womb onward. David prays to God in Psalm 51:5 words that apply to all of us: "Behold, I was brought forth in iniquity, and in sin did my mother conceive me." Behold, I, too, was born and conceived as David. You, I, and all people truly began to die on the day we were conceived. Every birthday party is but a reminder that so-and-so is walking straight toward the cold, dark grave. "Happy birthday, you're closer to death now than you were a year ago." That is the painful truth. We all were created by a good and gracious God, but we were created as children of a sinful mother and sinful father, whose own sinful mothers and fathers passed on to them the disease called original sin, which stems from our first parents—Adam and Eve. This "original sin," or "sin of origin," has its beginning, its origin, in the rebellion of Adam and Eve against the good Word of God. Their sin was not so much eating the fruit of the tree of the knowledge of good and evil, as much as it was not eating the Word of God. That is, rather than living "by every word that comes from the mouth of the LORD" (Deuteronomy 8:3), they chose to live by the lying words of Satan and the lying words of their own heart. The result was death, first spiritual death, and later physical death.

This condition, this "original leprosy" that we have inherited from a line of sinful moms and dads, stretches from the present all the way back to the Garden of Eden. As one of our hymns puts it: "In Adam we have all been one, One huge rebellious man; We all have fled that evening voice That sought us as we ran" (*Lutheran Worship* 292:1, © 1969 CPH). And this "one huge rebellious man" has leprosy covering every square inch of his body and soul.

Leprosy depicts our spiritual condition quite well. This disease does not remain hidden in the heart or liver or lungs like so many other illnesses. Leprosy manifests itself outwardly, publicly, for everyone to see. And so it is with sin. You cannot cover it up, no matter how hard you try. Sooner or later, it will be seen. No matter how beautiful or ugly you are, no matter how rich or poor, popular or unpopular, no matter your age, sex, or social class, the "leprosy" of sin clings to you. You cannot escape it.

Yes, *you* cannot escape it, but someone else can rescue you from it. The great physician of soul and body, our Lord Jesus Christ, has the only cure for leprosy. To Naaman He gave the cure for both physical and spiritual leprosy. To us He gives the cure for the leprosy of sin, a cure found in the medicinal waters of Holy Baptism.

You Get What You Pay For?

Read 2 Kings 5:2–5. From whom does Naaman learn of the prophet in Israel who can cure him? Discuss this girl's situation. Why is it so remarkable that she tries to help Naaman?

Naaman learned from an unlikely source that there was a prophet in Israel who would be able to heal him of his leprosy. "Now the Syrians on one of their raids had carried off a little girl from the land of Israel, and she worked in the service of Naaman's wife. She said to her mistress, 'Would that my lord were with the prophet who is in Samaria! He would cure him of his leprosy' " (2 Kings 5:2–3). What a confession of faith! This little girl—kidnapped, enslaved, separated from her family and friends in a foreign land—is the very one who speaks in love and truth to benefit her captor. Her confession is a good reminder of how God uses the words and actions of unexpected people to communicate His will and ways.

When Naaman traveled to Samaria, what did he take with him (2 Kings 5:5)? Discuss what this means. With what kind of mind-set does he approach the potential healing?

How is Naaman similar to people today (including us)? Do we really believe that God gives solely by grace? What are some ways we reveal our own lack of faith in God's free grace?

Naaman must have clung to the girl's words as the "Gospel truth" for he reported them to his king, who sent him to Israel to be cleansed. This leprous leader, however, did not go empty-handed. He took with him "ten talents of silver, six thousand shekels of gold, and ten changes of clothes" (5:5). If his servant girl was right, then surely he would have to pay dearly to be cured of his leprosy. Certainly he would have to "open his wallet" to obtain such a miraculous healing from the man of God. Good things don't come cheap. You get what you pay for, don't you?

No, you get what God gives! As St. Paul told the boastful Corinthians, "What do you have that you did not receive?" (1 Corinthians 4:7). The answer: nothing. God gives, we receive. As Hannah, the mother of Samuel, sang, "The Lord kills and brings to life; He brings down to Sheol and raises up. The Lord makes poor and makes rich; He brings low and He exalts" (1 Samuel 2:6–7). The Lord is the source of all healing, and that healing cannot be purchased.

Naaman's case is especially instructive. God healed him; Naaman had nothing to do with it. His healing is not a reward for seeking out God's prophet. His healing is not God's way of saying, "See what incentives I give for being obedient to Me!" No! Naaman deserved everything but healing. He is even stubborn about doing what God, through His prophet, instructs him to do. The leper adds nothing to what God does. The Lord gives him heal-

ing by grace and grace alone. He stretches out His healing hand to touch Naaman through the water of the Jordan River. It is a touch of love and mercy and compassion, a touch of the Holy One upon the unholy and unclean one. But that is the way of God, who purifies the unclean, forgives the sinner, and heals the sick. His will is to save and to bless—free of charge!

Looking for God in All the Wrong Places

Read 2 Kings 5:6–7. Where does Naaman first go when he arrives in Samaria? What is the king's reaction?

Read the story of the Wise Men in Matthew 2:1–12. How was their visit to Israel similar to Naaman's visit? What were they looking for? Where did they go first?

Having received a letter from his king to the king of Israel, and having packed his mules with lots of presents for the healer, Naaman set out for Samaria. But where was he supposed to go? Going to the king turned out to be the wrong choice. "And he brought the letter to the king of Israel, which read, 'When this letter reaches you, know that I have sent to you Naaman my servant, that you may cure him of his leprosy.' And when the king of Israel read the letter, he tore his clothes and said, 'Am I God, to kill and to make alive, that this man sends word to me to cure a man of his leprosy? Only consider, and see how he is seeking a quarrel with me'" (2 Kings 5:6–7).

As the king of Israel opened and read the letter, his jaw must have dropped open at the words "that you may cure him of his leprosy." The king understood the enormity of what was being asked. When he protests, "Am I God, to kill and to make alive?" he implicitly confesses the truth—God alone can heal this Syrian general standing before him. As was customary in that culture—to outwardly express the deep anger or sorrow one felt—the king tore his clothes. Surely, he thought, this outlandish request is nothing more than a scheming ploy from the king of Syria. He must be trying to start a fight with me by asking me to perform that which is humanly impossible.

Discuss why Naaman and the Wise Men are inclined to go to the king first. Why did they suppose God would be present there (either as the newborn king or as healer)? Were they associating God with the high and mighty or the low and common?

This is a good example of someone looking for God in the wrong place. Divine power to heal was not found in the king's palace, where one might expect it. It was not to be among the high and mighty that Naaman found the gracious presence of the healing God. Naaman was sent elsewhere. "When Elisha the man of God heard that the king of Israel had torn his clothes, he sent to the king, saying, 'Why have you torn your clothes? Let him come now to me, that he may know that there is a prophet in Israel' " (2 Kings 5:8).

"Let him come now to me," Elisha says. In other words, "Okay, Naaman, you've gone to the king, but he's not your man. Though powerful and royal, he will be of no help in receiving God's blessing. The Lord has located that help elsewhere. He has placed His healing word on my tongue. I am the prophet in Israel, God's 'mouth-man.' Come to me, and you'll come to God."

Looking for God in all the wrong places is one of the biggest problems we sinners have. We think we know where God can be found: in the awesome and in the powerful; in that which makes you feel good and "spiritual"; in that which we think is worthy of a heavenly, otherworldly Lord. Ah, but that's precisely our problem. We're looking for God where *we think* God should be, not where He has promised to be.

Naaman and we are very much like the Wise Men in this regard. Remember where they went first when they arrived in Israel, after having seen the star? Jerusalem, at the palace of the king. Where else would they go, right? Where else would the newborn king of Israel be but nestled in the soft, plush blankets of some palace crib with a silver spoon in His mouth?

But there He was not. He was not where they expected Him. He was in exactly the opposite place. He was not among the high, but the lowly; not among the rich, but the poor; not among the powerful, but among the powerless, the common, the ordinary. He was in the little town of Bethlehem.

Read 1 Corinthians 1:18–31. What do these verse tell you about the way God works? Where and in what does He choose to work? What is people's reaction to this? Why is God so hard to find if we are looking for Him where *we think* He should be?

Where do you look for God on earth? Where do you come to God, and where does God come to you? In what kinds of things does God locate His gifts of forgiveness, life, and salvation—healing from spiritual leprosy?

So it was with the Magi, so it was with Naaman, and so it still is with us. St. Paul tells us how God works and where He locates Himself: "But God chose what is foolish in the world to shame the wise; God chose what is weak in the world to shame the strong; God chose what is low and despised in the world, even things that are not, to bring to nothing things that are, so that no human being might boast in the presence of God" (1 Corinthians 1:27–29). In other words, God chose (and still chooses) to hide Himself behind masks that seem very "ungodlike"—not worthy of Him, much too common, ugly, despised.

What are the divine masks? A tiny baby wrapped in swaddling clothes, born in a barn; a bloody, naked man hanging from a cross; a sip of wine and bite of bread from the altar; a splash of water in the font. These are the masks of God: the Word and Sacraments. God is camouflaged in these, hiding behind them to do His work in your life.

A Disappointing Doctor's Visit

Read 2 Kings 5:9–12. Picture Naaman knocking on Elisha's door. What is all around him as he stands there? Do you get the impression that Naaman expected to be humbly received or something else?

When Naaman finally arrived at the home of the prophet Elisha, he must have thought at first that he had reached the end of the rainbow. Here the pot of gold—the remedy for his leprosy—would be waiting. "So Naaman came with his horses and chariots and stood at the door of Elisha's house" (2 Kings 5:9). There is more than a subtle hint of pride in this verse. There stands Naaman, the big-shot Syrian, surrounded by all the trappings of his wealth and power. His horses and chariots seem to say, "Wow, this fellow must be important—better pay attention to him, better give him top-notch service." That is clearly what Naaman was accustomed to receiving. He was, after all, not a lowly private in the Syrian armed forces. He had his conquests, his medallions, his stars. Naaman was the kind of man who *always* received the best.

Who comes to the door when Naaman arrives? What is his message? How are both of these answers an insult to Naaman? How does Naaman respond? What do his words reveal about his misunderstanding of the way God works?

Well, nearly always. But not this time! The balloon of pride needed to be popped before this patient was ready to see the doctor and receive the healing. "And Elisha sent a messenger to him, saying, 'Go and wash in the Jordan seven times, and your flesh shall be restored, and you shall be clean'" (2 Kings 5:10). This was a double insult to Naaman. First, the prophet himself did not come to inspect the leprosy; he sent a mere servant. Second, the method of healing was downright insane. Naaman blew his top: "Naaman was angry and went away, saying, 'Behold, I thought he would surely come out to me and stand and call upon the name of the LORD his God, and wave his hand over the place and cure the leper. Are not Abana and Pharpar, the rivers of Damascus, better than all the waters of Israel? Could I not wash in them and be clean?' So he turned and went away in a rage" (5:11–12).

Naaman clearly came to Samaria expecting to see something with outward showiness, something with pizzazz and excitement. Have you ever known someone who reacts similarly to where God is present to work healing today—in the Divine Service, in worship? How are these reactions parallel?

Temper, temper! You would have thought Elisha spit in Naaman's face. The insult, however, is even more deeply seated than that. What really "gets under Naaman's skin"? The fact that God's ways are not his ways. God is not conforming to the leper's expectations. He finds the whole situation unbelievable. The prophet stays inside. There's no hoopla whatsoever, no pizzazz, no fireworks, no waving of the hand. There is only a dirty river to wash in, a river far outdone by the rivers back home in Syria. Why, Naaman made this trip in vain if all he's supposed to do is go for a quick dip in the river. So he's mad, enraged at this foolish prophet, his foolish God, and his foolish means of healing.

The prophet of God offered Naaman a miracle that was disguised in simplicity. What kinds of "miracles disguised in simplicity" do God's prophets—His pastors today—offer? Are the saving power of the Word of God, Holy Baptism, and the Lord's Supper miraculous? How are these disguised in simplicity? How do people frequently react to them?

The crowds love showiness in religion. "Show me raw, awesome power. Show me razzle-dazzle. Show me signs and miracles." But that is not God's way. He specializes in miracles done undercover, done in simplicity. Our pride, like Naaman's pride, cannot accept that. We want the "peacock God" who struts His stuff. But the "peacock God" is an idol. It is not the true God.

Jesus certainly performed many miracles during His three-year ministry. He turned water into wine; corpses came back to life; and lepers were cleansed. But when He ascended, He left His church miracles that lack all showiness. He left Baptism, the Lord's Supper, Absolution, preaching. None of these produce a "Wow!" from the world. Indeed, very often, they produce a Naaman-like scoff at their earthiness.

But for those with eyes to see, the church does

indeed have miracles. Yes, every Sunday we have miracles. It is a miracle that a few words spoken over a sinner while water is poured over his head grants everlasting life and salvation. It is a miracle that a few words spoken over bread and wine place the very body and blood of the Lord Jesus into those earthly elements. It is a miracle that when the pastor says, "In the stead and by the command of my Lord Jesus Christ I forgive you . . ." that we really hear Jesus speak through the mouth of this man. It is a miracle that every Sunday Jesus Christ stands in the pulpit to preach—hidden within the pastoral office. It is a miracle veiled in simplicity and ordinariness.

As Elisha sent a simple servant with a simple medicine, so our Lord Jesus sends simple servants—His pastors—with simple medicine—the Word and Sacraments. All His gifts come wrapped in brown paper. But inside the wrapping is a pearl of great price, a treasure from God—His forgiveness, His life, His salvation.

Bowing to Simplicity

Read 2 Kings 5:13–14. Who finally convinces Naaman to do what the prophet says?

We've all had those moments when we flew into a rage over something, and while we were fuming, someone came to try and talk some sense into our troubled minds. Something like that happened with Naaman. Only his servants did not come to talk some sense into him, but to talk to him about receiving the gifts the Lord was offering, hidden in simplicity though they were. "His servants came near and said to him, 'My father, it is a great word the prophet has spoken to you; will you not do it? Has he actually said to you, "Wash, and be clean"?' " (2 Kings 5:13).

The Holy Spirit had given to the servants the eyes to see and the ears to hear that to which Naaman was blind and deaf. They heard the word of Elisha, which he spoke through his servant. The recognized it as "a great word," for it was a word that offered life to one caught up in death. It offered in

plain brown wrapping paper the priceless gift for which Naaman had made such a long journey. "Open it," they begged him. And Naaman finally believed. "So [Naaman] went down and dipped himself seven times in the Jordan, according to the word of the man of God, and his flesh was restored like the flesh of a little child, and he was clean" (2 Kings 5:14).

The Word of God finally had its way with Naaman, though it took a while and passed through many ears and out of many mouths before it took root in Naaman's own. God spoke it to Elisha; Elisha spoke it to his servant; his servant spoke it to Naaman; and Naaman's own servants spoke it to him again. It remained, however, the divine Word. It retained its own power to grant faith in the heart of the one who heard it and to grant healing in the waters to which it directed Naaman.

Discuss how Naaman's cleansing in the Jordan is the perfect illustration of the questions/answers in the Fourth Chief Part of the Small Catechism (The Sacrament of Holy Baptism). Use the language of the catechism to answer this question: *How can the Jordan's water do such great things?*

This part of the story is a perfect illustration of one of the questions and answers in the Small Catechism concerning Holy Baptism. There we read:

How can water do such great things? Certainly not just water, but the word of God in and with the water does these things, along with the faith which trusts this word of God in the water. For without God's word the water is plain water and no Baptism. But with the word of God it is a Baptism, that is, a life-giving water, rich in grace, and a washing of the new birth in the Holy Spirit. (Luther's Small Catechism)

Borrowing and adapting this language, we might ask, "How can *the Jordan water* do such great things *for Naaman*? Certainly not just *Jordan* water, but the Word of God *spoken by Elisha* in and with the water does these things, along with faith, which trusts this Word of God in the water. For without God's Word the water is plain water and no *cleansing*. But with the Word of God it is a *cleansing*, that is, a life-giving water, rich in grace, and a washing that *restored his flesh like the flesh of a little child.*

Water has no inherent power to save, to heal, to restore. Something must be added to it to fill it with a power not its own. That "something" is the Word of God. The very Word of God that created water is now added back to the water. The Word becomes wet—wet with grace, wet with mercy, wet with all the good things our Father wants to pour down upon His children.

Naaman was not baptized in the Jordan that day. But he was washed in water that was included in God's command and combined with God's Word. His was a forecast of Baptism, a sneak preview of what Jesus would give His church—the new and better Jordan in which we are born again and become as little children.

The Naaman in All of Us

There is a Naaman in all of us that doubts whether God's Word will really do what it promises, that rebels at God's simple ways, that wants razzle-dazzle in the things of God. But like Naaman, we are called to bow to divine simplicity. For God is not out to impress the world, but to save it and to save you. He carries us to the Jordan of the baptismal font, holds our leprous bodies over those cleansing waters, and splashes us with the saving bath done in His name. We are healed. We are cleansed. We find in the ordinary things of this world the extraordinary gifts of our Father who art in heaven.

Closing Prayer

Almighty God, heavenly Father, who healed leprous Naaman in the simple water of the Jordan River, grant that we, who are healed of the leprosy of sin in the waters of Holy Baptism, may ever remain covered by the cleansing waters of Your saving bath; through Jesus Christ, our Lord. Amen.

NaaMaN's "BaPtiSM" iN tHe JoRDaN

Too Simple

What is a common response to the complex problem of sin? Pinpoint various ways in which people try to "help God" by using their own strength, wisdom, willpower, and so forth to escape from sin.

Naaman's Problem

Read **2 Kings 5:1–5.** What kind of man was Naaman. Was he an Israelite? What was his nationality? What kind of relationship did the Israelites usually have with those outside their own nation?

What might Naaman's life have been like? Where would he likely have been on the social "totem pole"? At the top or bottom? What was his vocation? Does he seem to have a weak or a strong personality?

What was Naaman's problem? How might this problem have "handicapped" Naaman socially, politically, and militarily?

Naaman's health problem may not have been—strictly speaking—what we call "leprosy" (the Hebrew word used is a general word for many types of skin disease). However, whatever it was, it was certainly serious. Suppose, however, that it was leprosy. Look up the word *leprosy* in a dictionary or encyclopedia. What are the characteristics of this skin disease? What does it do to the body?

Discuss how Naaman's physical sickness is similar to our spiritual sickness—sin. How are they similar? What effects do they have on the body and soul?

Read **Psalm 51:5.** Do we become sinners, or are we conceived as sinners? Are adults and infants, therefore, sinners? What does this say about the need for the Baptism of people of all ages, including children?

You Get What You Pay For?

Read **2 Kings 5:2–5**. From whom does Naaman learn of the prophet in Israel who can cure him? Discuss this girl's situation. Why is it so remarkable that she tries to help Naaman?

When Naaman traveled to Samaria, what did he take with him? Discuss what this means. With what kind of mind-set does he approach the potential healing?

How is Naaman similar to people today (including us)? Do we really believe that God gives solely by grace? What are some ways we reveal our own lack of faith in God's free grace?

Looking for God in All the Wrong Places

Read **2 Kings 5:6–7**. Where does Naaman first go when he arrives in Samaria? What is the king's reaction?

Read the story of the Wise Men in **Matthew 2:1–12**. How was their visit to Israel similar to Naaman's visit? What were they looking for? Where did they go first?

Discuss why Naaman and the Wise Men are inclined to go to the king first. Why did they suppose God would be present there (either as the newborn king or as healer)? Were they associating God with the high and mighty or the low and common?

Read **1 Corinthians 1:18–31**. What do these verse tell you about the way God works? Where and in what does He choose to work? What is people's reaction to this? Why is God so hard to find if we are looking for Him where *we think* He should be?

Where do you look for God on earth? Where do you come to God, and where does God come to you? In what kinds of things does God locate His gifts of forgiveness, life, and salvation—healing from spiritual leprosy?

A Disappointing Doctor's Visit

Read **2 Kings 5:9–12**. Picture Naaman knocking on Elisha's door. What is all around him as he stands there? Do you get the impression that Naaman expected to be humbly received or something else?

Who comes to the door when Naaman arrives? What is his message? How are both of these answers an insult to Naaman? How does Naaman respond? What do his words reveal about his misunderstanding of the way God works?

Naaman clearly came to Samaria expecting to see something with outward showiness, something with pizzazz and excitement. Have you ever known someone who reacts similarly to where God is present to work healing today—in the Divine Service, in worship? How are these reactions parallel?

The prophet of God offered Naaman a miracle that was disguised in simplicity. What kinds of "miracles disguised in simplicity" do God's prophets—His pastors today—offer? Are the saving power of the Word of God, Holy Baptism, and the Lord's Supper miraculous? How are these disguised in simplicity? How do people frequently react to them?

Bowing to Simplicity

Read **2 Kings 5:13–14.** Who finally convinces Naaman to do what the prophet says?

One of the questions/answers in the Fourth Chief Part of the Small Catechism (The Sacrament of Holy Baptism) reads as follows:

How can water do such great things? *Certainly not just water, but the word of God in and with the water does these things, along with the faith which trusts this word of God in the water. For without God's word the water is plain water and no Baptism. But with the word of God it is a Baptism, that is, a life-giving water, rich in grace, and a washing of the new birth in the Holy Spirit.* (Luther's Small Catechism)

Discuss how Naaman's cleansing in the Jordan is the perfect illustration of these words. Use the language of the catechism to answer this question: *How can the Jordan's water do such great things?*

THE BAPTISM OF JESUS

Lesson Focus

When Jesus was baptized in the Jordan River, all humanity was funneled into the body of Jesus. All of humanity got wet. Every man, woman, and child who has lived, does live, and will live stood in those waters that day. He is baptized for them. He fulfills all righteousness for them. He keeps the Law for them. In the same way that He resisted the devil's temptations for all, died for all, and rose for all, so He was baptized for all.

Opening Prayer

Father in heaven, as at the baptism in the Jordan River, You once proclaimed Jesus Your beloved Son and anointed Him with the Holy Spirit, grant that all who are baptized in His name may faithfully keep the covenant into which they have been called, boldly confess their Savior, and with Him be heirs of life eternal; through Jesus Christ, who lives and reigns with You and the Holy Spirit, one God, now and forever. Amen (Collect for the Baptism of Our Lord, *Lutheran Worship*, p. 21).

Not Just Plain Water

Ask participants to take some time to reflect on the common water themes that have been covered in the sessions thus far. Note three or four key similarities between the various Old Testament stories that involve water. How has water been used? For whom has it been used? Has water been associated primarily with good or bad things, cursing or blessing?

We have studied several Old Testament stories in which water is central. In these stories we have observed time and time again how God uses this liquid to fuse the Old Testament and New Testament together. There is the water of creation and the Garden of Eden, the water that caused Noah's ark to float, the water that drowned Pharaoh with all his army in the Red Sea, and the water of the Jordan River that cleansed Naaman the leper. Truth be told, in these stories we've only begun to scratch the surface! There is a whole ocean of other examples we could dive into, if only we had the time. You certainly have a good idea of the centrality of water in the bib-

lical story. You can hardly turn a page in the Scriptures without getting wet!

In this lesson we will jump from the Old Testament to the New. However, this "jump" is not over a huge canyon. In fact, moving from the Old Testament to the New Testament is not so much a jump as a half-step—where part of your foot is still in the Old Testament and part of it is in the New Testament. Water clearly unites the Old and New Testaments.

Unless we look at the New Testament use of water in Baptism in light of the Old Testament's use of water, we will be far from seeing the *whole* truth of Baptism. Viewing Baptism apart from the use of water in the Old Testament is like viewing something with one eye closed—you get only half the picture. Baptismal water, if we are to see it with 20/20 vision, must be looked at with New Testament *and* Old Testament eyes.

When our Savior reveals that He will employ water as the part of creation to which He will join His saving Word, we are hardly surprised. How could we be? Hasn't God been using water all along

to bless His people with life, to sustain them in their travels, to rescue them from their enemies, to kill that which is opposed to Him, to heal sinners of their sicknesses?

Therefore, the water of Baptism is not just plain water. The Word of God in that water makes it "a life-giving water, rich in grace, and a washing of the new birth in the Holy Spirit" (Small Catechism). But baptismal water is not just plain water for another reason as well: the Old Testament Word has been intimately joined to it. By the time you read all the way through the Old Testament to the Gospels, water is already flooded with importance and saturated with stories of salvation. The account of the baptism of Jesus is a New Testament painting in which the artist dipped his brush into the "water colors" of the Old Testament.

Jordan River: Same Song, Final Verse

The Jordan River is part of the story of Israel herself. Briefly review the history recorded in Joshua 1–5. Where had Israel been before

59

Joshua 1? What was the nation about to encounter when she crossed over into the land of Canaan? Was this land populated or unpopulated? How would it be possible for them to conquer it (Joshua 2:9)?

The Jordan River is more than a geographical marker of the boundary between Israel and her neighbors to the east. This river is part of the story of Israel herself. You cannot relate Israel's story without talking a whole lot about the Jordan. Not that it is a magnificently beautiful river or astounding in size. Actually, it's not much to look at. Naaman turned up his nose at the Jordan, pronouncing it to be far inferior to the rivers of Damascus (2 Kings 5:12). The Jordan's beauty or ugliness, largeness or smallness, has nothing to do with its importance. It is important because of what God did there—the beautiful, astounding act of salvation He performed there for His church.

Jesus began His ministry of conquering sin and death in the very river in which Israel began her conquest of the Promised Land. After 40 years of wandering in the wilderness, following the death of Moses and Aaron and all but two of the adults who had left bondage in Egypt, the nation of Israel stood on the eastern bank of the Jordan River. On the western side of this river lay the land God had promised to give Abraham, Isaac, and Jacob. It was the land often described as "flowing with milk and honey" (Exodus 3:8, 17; 13:5; etc.). But it was also flowing—actually bubbling over—with enemy nations. Israel did not stare across the Jordan's waters into an uninhabited paradise, but into a populated piece of real estate. The coming conquest would certainly not be like taking candy from a baby; indeed, it would be more like wrestling raw meat from the fangs of a wolf!

Wolfish nations though there be, one truth made all the difference: God was on Israel's side. The church had His Word of promise never to leave them, never to forsake them, but to be with them and to fight for them against their enemies. For what more could they ask?

Israel first had to cross the Jordan before beginning the conquest of Canaan. What time of year was this (Joshua 3:15)? Was the river at its high or low point? How did this present even more of a challenge to the nation?

How did the nation cross the Jordan River (Joshua 3)? What piece of "holy furniture" was central in the crossing? What purpose did the ark serve in the tabernacle (Exodus 25:10–22)? With what does David compare the ark (1 Chronicles 28:2)? How is Jesus our new "ark of the covenant"?

First, Israel had to get across the Jordan River. This was no easy task, so it seemed, given the fact that it was springtime and the river was overflowing its banks (Joshua 3:15). How were they to cross the water safely? How were they to get to the land the Lord would give them? The Lord God of Israel had the answer, an answer that gives you more than a little déjà vu: He would part the waters so that Israel would pass through on dry ground. It would be the Red Sea all over again! Only this time Israel would not be fleeing from her enemies to enter a wilderness; she would be crossing over to face her enemies in the land flowing with milk and honey.

The account of the crossing is recorded in Joshua 3. When the priests who carried the ark of the covenant set foot in the Jordan River, the waters split, dry ground emerged, and Israel walked into the land of their inheritance. Led by Joshua, the church began her gradual conquest of the Promised Land.

Joshua is a Hebrew name that means "Yahweh is salvation." If we wrote "Joshua" in Greek, it would be spelled "Jesus." Thus, our Lord Jesus and Joshua share the same name. This is no mere coincidence. How is Jesus our new and better Joshua? If Joshua led Israel in the conquest of the enemy, whom has our new and better Joshua conquered? Whom did He face immediately after He was baptized (Matthew 4:1–11)?

It would be many centuries (14 to be exact!) before another "Joshua" would stand on the bank of this same Jordan River in preparation for battles ahead. Jesus—whose Hebrew name is Joshua—

came to these waters to be baptized. He could have chosen a pool in Jerusalem; He could have chosen any number of rivers or streams in Israel; He could have gone anywhere to be baptized. But He was not acting willy-nilly. His was a set purpose, a purpose understandable only from the perspective of the Old Testament. Just as He did not come merely to be sacrificed, but to be sacrificed *in Jerusalem*, even so He did not come merely to be baptized, but to be baptized *in the Jordan*. Location meant a great deal. In choosing specific locations, Jesus connected Himself to the Old Testament history of salvation and showed its fulfillment in Himself.

Jesus is baptized in the Jordan as our Joshua who comes to battle sin and death in order to acquire for us an eternal inheritance in the heavenly Promised Land. Indeed, immediately after He is baptized, Jesus goes into the wilderness for a 40-day battle with the tempter (Matthew 4:1–11). A coincidence? Hardly! If Israel had to wrestle raw meat from the fangs of a wolf, then Jesus faced an ever greater challenge: He would wrestle humanity—you—from the fangs of the wolf of hell. The satanic wolf, who had held Adam and his descendants in his teeth since Eden, would now face the Shepherd who would take Adam back. The wolf would be defeated, life would be won, and this all for you.

John: Priest, Prophet, and Baptizer

Read Matthew 3:1–6. John the Baptist was a unique individual. What set John apart? How was he different?

There was another reason Jesus came to the Jordan River to be baptized: along these waters was where the "baptizer," John the Baptist, was doing his work. What a strange character! John is one of those unusual biblical personalities that we modern people shake our heads at. We just cannot figure him out—his clothing (camel's hair), his diet (grasshoppers and honey), and his favorite word in preaching ("Repent!"). All these words grate against our modern sensitivities. Let's be honest: John is uncivilized. A man with grasshopper legs stuck

between his teeth would never make the cover of *GQ!*

Yes, John has—what shall we call them—"unique character traits"? But these were not accidental. In fact, they were of God's own design. John was not an eccentric adult who never really outgrew his rebellious teenage years! He is who he is, and he does what he does in fulfillment of the divine plan. If we wish to understand why John baptized Jesus—or, rather, why the Father baptized Jesus *through* John—we need to explore these "unique character traits."

Read Luke 1:5–25. John was from a priestly family. In fact, his father, Zechariah, was burning incense and praying in the temple when the angel Gabriel told Zechariah that he would be John's father. A normal priest, however, served at the temple in Jerusalem. Where was John's "temple"? What kind of unusual "vestments" did John wear? What kind of language did John the priest use to describe Jesus (see John 1:29)? Why was this particularly appropriate for a priest to say?

To begin with, John is actually an Israelite priest. In the Old Testament the male descendants of Aaron (the brother of Moses) served as priests (Exodus 28). This was the line from which John was born. In fact, his priestly father, Zechariah, was burning incense in the temple and praying for the nation when the archangel Gabriel announced to him that Elizabeth, his wife, would become pregnant with a son. John's priestly ministry, however, was not in the temple at Jerusalem; it was in the "wilderness temple." The Jordan River was his tabernacle, altar, and holy place.

Read Luke 1:16–17, 76–79. John was not only a priest, but was also a prophet. As a prophet, what was he to do? With which OT prophet was John compared?

Compare 2 Kings 1:8 with Matthew 3:4. What outward similarity existed between these two men?

On the eighth day of his life, when John was circumcised and named, his father, Zechariah, sang of him: "And you, child, will be called the prophet of the Most High; for you will go before the Lord to prepare His ways" (Luke 1:76). This was in fulfillment of the prophecy of Malachi, who foretold John's coming with these words: "Behold, I will send you Elijah the prophet before the great and awesome day of the LORD comes" (Malachi 4:5; see also Isaiah 40:3–5). John came "in the spirit and power of Elijah" (Luke 1:17) to preach to the people of Israel, to call them to repentance, to Baptism, and to faith in the Messiah.

That he came "in the spirit and power of Elijah" explains John's unique clothing: "a garment of camel's hair and a leather belt around his waist" (Matthew 3:4). John wore this kind of garment to link his ministry with that of Elijah, who also "wore a garment of hair, with a belt of leather around his waist" (2 Kings 1:8). But their similar wardrobe was not the only connection between these two prophets. Elijah preached during a time in Israel's history when there was a great falling away from God and His Word. John ministered in a similar situation. He, like Elijah before him, came "to turn the hearts of the fathers to the children, and the disobedient to the wisdom of the just, to make ready for the Lord a people prepared" (Luke 1:17; Malachi 4:6).

> **What two foods were evidently central in the diet of John the Baptist (Matthew 3:4)? What were locusts associated with in the Old Testament (see Exodus 10:1–20)? What was honey associated with in the Old Testament (see Exodus 3:8, 17)? Out of John's mouth proceeded words that threatened God's judgment against unbelief (Luke 3:7–9) as well as promised blessings in the Messiah (Luke 1:76–79; John 1:29–34). How might John's diet be symbolic of the two messages of his preaching?**

A word must also be mentioned about John's rather unusual diet of locusts (or grasshoppers, as we commonly call them) and wild honey. This prophet's meals were to some extent a symbol of his ministry. In the Old Testament grasshoppers were intimately associated with divine wrath that came in the form of plagues (e.g., Exodus 10:1–20).

Honey, on the other hand, was associated with blessings, just as Canaan was called the land "flowing with milk and honey." Out of John's mouth would come words that declared two realities: the coming divine wrath that would befall those who rejected God's Messiah (locusts) and the sweet blessings of life that believers would receive in the Messiah (honey). In other words, John preached Law and Gospel, threat and grace, "locusts and honey." What John put into his mouth was indicative of what came out of his mouth.

What came out of John's mouth is summarized in one phrase: "Repent, for the kingdom of heaven is at hand" (Matthew 3:2). To repent is not merely to feel sorry for doing something wrong. Repentance is not an occasional emotion but a constant motion—a movement from sin to grace, death to life, the devil to Jesus. To repent is to live in ongoing confession of sins and faith in Christ's word of forgiveness. The kingdom of heaven (or "the kingdom of God") is the gracious reign of our Father, through Jesus Christ, in His Spirit, over His church. John announced this coming kingdom—a kingdom of mercy, forgiveness, and everlasting life found in the One to whom John pointed and said, "Behold, the Lamb of God, who takes away the sin of the world" (John 1:29).

> **John's preaching was accompanied by his baptizing. John the Baptist simply means "John the Baptizer." This close link between ministry and water is similar to other OT men. How was water associated with Noah, Moses, and Joshua?**

John—the wilderness priest, the "prophet like Elijah," the preacher of "locusts and honey"—is also the *baptist* (a word that simply means "one who baptizes"—John the Baptizer, we might call him). This close connection of water with a man's ministry is something new in biblical history. It is only *relatively* new, however, since water had certainly been associated with the ministry of Noah, Moses, Joshua, the priests, and others. None of them had been called a "baptizer," but their ministry had certainly been linked with water. Moreover, this close connection is also only relatively new because the

Jews in the first century B.C. and A.D. had already been practicing a sort of "baptism." When Gentiles (non-Jews) were converted by the Holy Spirit and confessed faith in the God of Israel, the males were circumcised, and all Gentiles underwent a ritual bath. This ritual bath, or "baptism," was understood to wash away their old, pagan way of life. Thus when John began to baptize in the Jordan River, the Jews did not have to ask, "What in the world if this fellow up to—washing people in the water?" The people of Israel knew all about the sacred use of water from their own biblical history, and they knew all about a ritual bath to wash away sins.

Therefore, when Jesus came to the Jordan to be baptized by John, He came to the man whom God especially ordained for this purpose. If Adam is the A of Old Testament history, then John is the Z. But he is not just the final chapter, he is also the summary chapter. John is the last of the Old Testament prophets, the final Old Testament priest, the Old Testament preacher who wraps everything up and hands it to the Messiah for filling and fulfilling.

Jesus Puts Himself into the Water

The baptism of Jesus is described in various ways by all four evangelists. Read their accounts in Matthew 3:13–17; Mark 1:9–11; Luke 3:21–22; John 1:29–34. What are the unique features of each account? What are the similarities?

Many people have wondered, and still wonder, why Jesus was baptized. You have to admit that, on the surface, it does not seem to make sense. If Baptism is for the forgiveness of sins (Mark 1:4), and if Jesus is without sin, then why does He need to be baptized? Why would one who is not "dirty with sin" need this cleansing bath? These good questions lead us to the very heart of the Gospel, to the very reason why Jesus came.

To answer the question "Why was Jesus baptized?" we need to take a close look at the short dialogue between John and Jesus that occurs right before Jesus' baptism. Second, we need to explore the meaning of the various wonders that accompanied His baptism.

Matthew records the hesitancy of John the Baptist when Jesus comes to be baptized by him. What does John say? What is the basis of his protest?

How does Jesus respond to John? Take some time to dwell on the words of Jesus' response.

Matthew records for us the words exchanged between John and Jesus on that momentous day, as well as the heavenly and earthly wonders that happened when Jesus was baptized.

Then Jesus came from Galilee to the Jordan to John, to be baptized by him. John would have prevented Him, saying, "I need to be baptized by You, and do You come to me?" But Jesus answered him, "Let it be so now, for thus it is fitting for us to fulfill all righteousness." Then he consented. And when Jesus was baptized, immediately He went up from the water, and behold, the heavens were opened to Him, and He saw the Spirit of God descending like a dove and coming to rest on Him; and behold, a voice from heaven said, "This is My beloved Son, with whom I am well pleased." (Matthew 3:13–17)

John the Baptist is clearly hesitant to baptize the man who stands before him. "John would have prevented Him," for it seemed to him that the tables should be turned. To be sure, God had sent John to baptize, but He sent him to baptize sinners to prepare them for the coming of the Messiah. How could he baptize the Messiah? Indeed, John knows his own unworthiness, his own iniquity, as well as the innocence and worthiness of Jesus. "I need to be baptized by You," John protests.

"Let it be so *now*," Jesus says (Matthew 3:15). Our Lord focuses on the fact that "now" is the time. Compare this "now-ness" of Jesus' response with the words in Galatians 4:4 about the "fullness of time."

The response of Jesus to John's protest of his own guilt and Jesus' innocence is this: "Let it be so now, for thus it is fitting for us to fulfill all righteousness." Our Lord begins to answer John by saying, "Let it be so *now* . . ." It is the word *now* that is significant in this phrase. Jesus was saying, "Baptize Me now, John, for now is the day of salvation; now is the day for which all creation has been waiting since the fall of Adam and Eve; now will be accomplished that of which all the prophets preached; now have I, the Anointed One, come to do My Father's will; yes, John, now is the day."

Jesus concludes, "to fulfill all righteousness" (verse 15). What is righteousness? How does Jesus fulfill all righteousness for all people? To what does Isaiah compare our righteousness (Isaiah 64:6)?

Read Romans 4. By what do we receive the righteousness of God?

Jesus goes on to say, "For thus it is fitting for us to fulfill all righteousness." Jesus is telling John, "When you baptize Me, this will be fitting, it will be appropriate, it will be in entire conformity with the will of God. For this baptism is the way we will fulfill all righteousness. All that is lacking in the righteousness of sinners; all their inability to fulfill My Law; all the holiness they do not have, the perfection they do not have, the innocence they do not have—all of these things that are lacking in them will be replaced. When you baptize Me, we will fill them to the full with holiness, innocence, perfection, and righteousness. This is the Father's will, plan, and salvation—that you baptize Me."

Jesus also says "for us." What does Jesus mean by "us"? Does He mean Himself and John? Or does He mean Himself, the Father, and the Spirit?

Is there anything Jesus did not fulfill for us? Think about how Jesus passed through every stage of our life—from infancy to adulthood—and all the while kept God's Law perfectly. Is the Gospel only that Jesus died and rose for you? How is the life of Jesus also Good News for you?

But how could the baptism of Jesus do and provide all these things? When Jesus is baptized, He

steps into the place of sinners. John is exactly right—he himself needed baptism, not Jesus. But that is why our Lord came: to do for us what we needed, not what He needed. He came to be born for us, live for us, be baptized for us, suffer for us, die for us, rise for us, and ascend for us. Every "for us" that Jesus did was done in our stead, in our place. He wears our flesh and stands in our shoes to do all these things and to have them done to Him. He is our substitute, not just on the cross, but in everything from His nine months in the womb to His three days in the tomb.

This is the way Jesus fulfills all righteousness—by filling our own lives to the full with His own works. Since every part of our lives is polluted by unrighteousness, then Jesus goes through every part of our lives—doing what we do—only doing it perfectly. We are conceived in sin; he is conceived without sin. We are born sinful; He, sinless. We live lives of Law-breaking; He, Law-keeping. We suffer and complain; He endures it silently. Every step we take, every breath we breathe, Jesus does also, filling with His perfection what is filled with our own imperfection. This He does for all the world.

In the Jordan River that day all humanity was funneled into the body of Jesus. When He was baptized, all of humanity got wet. Every man, woman, and child who has lived, does live, and will live stood in those waters that day. He is baptized for them. He fulfills all righteousness for them. He keeps the Law for them. In the same way that He resisted the devil's temptations for all, died for all, and rose for all, so He was baptized for all.

How many baptisms does Ephesians 4:5–6 say there are? Discuss this statement: "Indeed, you could rightly say that there has really been only one Baptism ever: the baptism of Jesus. Every other Baptism is not a repetition of Jesus', but an incorporation into His."

Indeed, you could rightly say that there has really been only one Baptism ever—the baptism of Jesus. Every other Baptism is *not* a repetition of His, but an incorporation into His. We are baptized into His baptism. Every Baptism is but a stream that empties into the ocean of Jesus' baptism. Thus Paul says there is "One Lord, one faith, *one baptism*, one God and Father of all, who is over all and through all and in all" (Ephesians 4:5–6).

Jesus is baptized, therefore, not because we are sinful, but because He came to save sinners. He puts Himself into the water in order that through the water He might put Himself into you. He—as it were—baptizes the water with His body so that through water you might be placed into His body. He fulfills all righteousness for all the unrighteous. He does it all for you.

The Heavenly Veil Is Opened

What happens when Jesus comes out of the Jordan River?

Matthew not only records the conversation between Jesus and John on the day of our Lord's baptism, but he also records three wonders that accompanied that act: the opening of the heavens, the descent of the Spirit like a dove, and the voice of the Father. Each wonder underlines the reason for the baptism of Jesus, as well as demonstrates the way in which this story is fused with several Old Testament stories.

Regarding the first, Matthew writes: "And when Jesus was baptized, immediately He went up from the water, and behold, the heavens were opened to Him" (Matthew 3:16). How exactly were the heavens opened? What was the purpose of this opening? Are they still open? Questions such as these are raised by this wonder.

Compare this miracle with the vision of Ezekiel in Ezekiel 1. What are some similarities? Beside what kind of body of water do both miracles happen? What does Ezekiel see in 1:26–28? What kind of form does God have in this appearance?

"Opening the heavens" is the Old Testament way of saying that God is about to make Himself known to His people. The premier example of this is in the vision of the prophet Ezekiel. He describes his vision of the appearance of God to him with these words: "In the thirtieth year, in the fourth month on the fifth day, while I was among the exiles by the Kebar River, the heavens were opened and I saw visions of God" (Ezekiel 1:1 NIV). What is especially important about Ezekiel's vision beside the river is in the climax of the account.

Above the expanse over their heads was what looked like a throne of sapphire, and high above on the throne was a figure like that of a man. I saw that from what appeared to be His waist up He looked like glowing metal, as if full of fire, and that from there down He looked like fire; and brilliant light surrounded Him. Like the appearance of a rainbow in the clouds on a rainy day, so was the radiance around Him. This was the appearance of the likeness of the glory of the LORD. *When I saw it, I fell facedown, and I heard the voice of one speaking. (Ezekiel 1:26–28 NIV)*

What this prophet views is astounding: seated on (what is commonly called) the chariot throne of God was " a figure like that of a man." God *in the form of a man* appears to Ezekiel when the heavens are opened. Furthermore, this God in the form "of a man" is none other than "the likeness of the glory of the LORD," the very same glory that was often connected with the appearance of the Son of God in the Old Testament.

When you compare this vision with Jesus' baptism, the parallel is astounding: the God who appeared to Ezekiel in "a figure like that of a man" while he was by the Kebar River (Chebar in ESV) is now standing as a true man on the banks of the Jordan River! To Ezekiel He appeared as a regal figure on a throne, but here He appears as a king camouflaged in humility.

Is it correct to say that when we see Jesus we *actually see God* (John 1:18; 14:9)?

The heavens are thus opened at the baptism of Jesus so that we can see that God has come down in Jesus Christ to make Himself known as a true man. When we want to see God, we look at the God-man Jesus, for He is God in the flesh. As Jesus Himself says, "Whoever has seen Me has seen the Father" (John 14:9). Or, as St. John testifies earlier in his Gospel: "No one has ever seen God; the only

God, who is at the Father's side, He has made Him known" (John 1:18). No one has ever seen God the Father, but the only-begotten God, Jesus Christ, has made Him known. He is the revelation of who God is for "in Him the whole fullness of deity dwells bodily" (Colossians 2:9). What Ezekiel saw as God only *appearing* to have flesh and blood we see as the everlasting reality: the Son of God has assumed our human nature from the Virgin Mary so that He is "true God, begotten of the Father from eternity and also true man, born of the Virgin Mary" (Small Catechism).

Understood in this way, the opening of the heavens that day beside the Jordan River was not a temporary crack in the celestial door but a permanent opening. It is permanent insofar as Jesus is the permanent revelation of the Father. In Him, we today still see the God who wears our skin, who has made our human flesh and blood His own. And just as at the Jordan River, He once manifested Himself as the One who has come down from heaven, so at our Baptism He still manifests Himself as that One. He has come down from heaven and been made man so that we might be baptized into His body, thereby becoming one with Him.

The Spirit's Dove

Read Genesis 1:1–2. When the Holy Spirit descended upon Jesus, He did so in the form of a dove. Elsewhere in the Bible, the Holy Spirit is described as a dove or as hovering as a dove might do. What is the Spirit doing? Over what is He hovering?

Compare this with the baptism of Jesus in light of 2 Corinthians 5:17. Paul says that if we are in Jesus we are a new creation. Discuss how the baptism of Jesus is like a re-Genesis of the world.

The second wonder that happened on the day of Jesus' baptism was the coming of the Holy Spirit. Matthew records this wonder with these words: "[Jesus] saw the Spirit of God descending like a dove and coming to rest on Him" (Matthew 3:16).

St. John expands on these words with this description:

> The next day he saw Jesus coming toward him, and said, "Behold, the Lamb of God, who takes away the sin of the world! This is He of whom I said, 'After me comes a man who ranks before me, because He was before me.' I myself did not know Him, but for this purpose I came baptizing with water, that He might be revealed to Israel." And John bore witness: "I saw the Spirit descend from heaven like a dove, and it remained on Him. I myself did not know Him, but He who sent me to baptize with water said to me, 'He on whom you see the Spirit descend and remain, this is He who baptizes with the Holy Spirit.' And I have seen and have borne witness that this is the Son of God." (John 1:29–34)

Among other things, John bears witness to that fact that the Spirit remains on Jesus, that Jesus is the Son of God, and that He baptizes with this Holy Spirit.

The chief question we want to consider is why the Spirit descends in the form of a dove. For what reason did the Spirit choose this particular way of appearing visibly, and why would He choose this particular bird? Was this simply one choice among many? Could He have appeared as a rabbit, a lion, or a lamb?

Read Genesis 8:8–12. What place does the dove have in the account of the Flood and Noah's ark? How is this dove a bearer of good news? What kind of good news? In what way is the Holy Spirit's coming in the form of a dove also good news? From what kind of "flood" are we rescued by being baptized into Jesus (see 2 Peter 3:5–7)?

Of course, the Holy Spirit *could have appeared* in many forms, but He did not. He chose to appear not only as a bird, but as a particular kind of bird—a dove. Why? The connection between this dove and the dove Noah released from the ark comes to mind. Toward the end of Noah's many months on the ark he released a raven, which "went to and fro until the waters were dried up from the earth" (Genesis 8:7). Thus, the raven would not be a bearer of good news. His constant circling in the sky said only one thing: "These waters of punishment are still covering the face of the earth." Then, Noah released another bird:

> He sent forth a dove from him, to see if the waters had subsided from the face of the ground. But the dove found no place to set her foot, and she returned to him to the ark, for the waters were still on the face of the whole earth. So he put out his hand and took her and brought her into the ark with him. He waited another seven days, and again he sent forth the dove out of the ark. And the dove came back to him in the evening, and behold, in her mouth was a freshly plucked olive leaf. So Noah knew that the waters had subsided from the earth. Then he waited another seven days and sent forth the dove, and she did not return to him anymore. (Genesis 8:8–12)

Unlike the raven, the dove became the bearer of good news. The second time it was sent out, the dove returned with an olive leaf, bearing witness to the fact that vegetation had begun to grow for "the waters had subsided from the earth." The third time the dove was released, she did not return, indicating that she had found a dry and secure place to land.

How is the Holy Spirit involved in your Baptism (Titus 3:4–5)? What does your body become when you are baptized (1 Corinthians 3:16; 6:19)?

That dove of Noah, bearer of good news that it was, served as a preview of the dove of the Spirit. The Holy Spirit clothed Himself in the form of a dove to alight upon Jesus at His baptism so that this good news might be sent: "This Son of God will bring an end to the wrath of God that has swamped this world like a flood. He who is wet now with baptismal water will be flooded with the divine judgment against the world's sin. The waters of wrath will subside from the earth, for they will be funneled into Him, into His body as He bears your sins on the tree of the cross. He will thus become your peace, the One who reconciles God and man."

The dove of the Spirit, therefore, along with the heavens opening and the dialogue between John and Jesus, explain the reason Jesus is baptized and what happens at your Baptism. The heavens open

for you; the righteousness of Jesus is placed upon you; the dove of the Spirit permanently lands upon you. In fact, the Spirit dwells within you. God the Father does all this on your behalf. He does all this in the saving water of the heavenly fountain.

The Heavenly Voice

What does the Father say from heaven when Jesus is baptized?

The last, but certainly not least, part of the baptism of Jesus is the Father's short but powerful sermon that He preached on the day of His Son's baptism. Matthew records that when Jesus was baptized, "a voice from heaven said, 'This is My beloved Son, with whom I am well pleased' " (Matthew 3:17). These 11 words, like Baptism itself, are saturated not only with importance, but also with great comfort, for they testify to who Jesus is, who His Father is, and who and whose you are that are baptized into the body of Jesus.

Read Exodus 20:1–21. At Jesus' baptism the Father spoke from heaven. At Mount Sinai God also spoke from heaven. What was the people's reaction to God speaking? Compare what God spoke at Sinai with what God spoke at the Jordan River. How are these messages different?

At Sinai God spoke Ten Commandments, the Law. At the Jordan the Father identifies the Son, who came to do what with the Law (Matthew 5:17)?

"This is My beloved Son," the voice says. The very fact that God speaks from heaven is extraordinary. The most prominent occasion in prior biblical history when God spoke from heaven in a public setting was at Mount Sinai (Exodus 20). There His sermon was highly different from the one He delivered at the Jordan River. At Sinai, God did not say, "This is My beloved Son," but "Thou shalt . . . Thou shalt not." He spoke the Ten Commandments, literally the "10 words." The reaction of the people to God's speaking was great fear and trembling. They begged

Moses, "You speak to us, and we will listen; but do not let God speak to us, lest we die" (Exodus 20:19). These 10 words of Law demanded of them what they could not give—perfect obedience to the perfect will of the almighty Judge. No wonder they were frightened! No wonder they did not want God to speak to them directly again!

Contrast those 10 words of Law at Sinai with the 11 words of Gospel at the Jordan. The Law requires what the people cannot give, but the Gospel only gives, only blesses. "This is My beloved Son, with whom I am well pleased." Here there are no "Thou shalts" or "Thou shalt nots," only "This is." The Father is saying, "This is My beloved Son, the One who will keep the Law for you, fulfill its demands perfectly for you, and even suffer its penalty for your transgression of it." This is Good News indeed!

In His heavenly sermon the Father could have identified Jesus in any number of ways. He could have said, "This is My Servant," as Jesus is called in several prophecies in Isaiah (42:1; 49:3; 52:13). He could have called Him the Promised One, the Messiah, the King of Israel, or any one of a number of titles. But the Father identifies Jesus as His Son, and not only His Son, but His *beloved* Son.

"Son" is more than a title when spoken of Jesus. It is who Jesus is, not the office He holds. In other words, to be called "Son" is far different from being called King, Savior, or Shepherd. These titles are all related to what the Son does: He rules as King, rescues as Savior, guides and protects as a Shepherd. But Jesus *is* the Son of God. He does not become Son, is not made Son, but is eternally Son. As long as God is Father, so long is Jesus the Son—from all eternity.

He is the *beloved* Son for He is the One on whom the Father has placed His love. "God is love," says St. John (1 John 4:8). If God *is* love, then He is love from all eternity. That means that God must have been loving someone forever. But whom could God love from all eternity? Whom could He love before He created the world? No one else but the Son (and the Spirit as well). "The Father loves the Son" (John 3:35; 5:20). Thus St. Paul simply calls

Jesus "the Beloved" (Ephesians 1:6). That says it all.

And not only does the Father love the Son, but He is also well pleased with Him. There is nothing lacking in the Son; He is nothing less than exactly as the Father would have Him be. The Father rejoices in this Son whom He has sent for He is doing the will of the Father—saving us from our sins, fulfilling all righteousness for us, standing in our place under the Law to keep it, and suffering its judgment for our iniquities.

Jesus is the Son of God by nature. He is "God of God, Light of Light, very God of very God." He is the Son of God from all eternity. The Scriptures, however, also refer to the baptized as "sons of God" (Romans 8:14). What image does Paul use in Galatians 3:27 to describe our close connection to Jesus in Baptism? Read Romans 8:15. There Paul says that we became the sons of God by adoption.

Review and discuss the Fourth Chief Part of Luther's Small Catechism. How does the study of Jesus' baptism further help to answer many of the questions in this part of the Catechism?

The fact that *at His baptism* Jesus is called "My Son" and "beloved" and the One in whom God is "well pleased" is of tremendous comfort for us. For what happens to us when we are baptized? We are "all baptized into one body" (1 Corinthians 12:13). We are "baptized into Christ Jesus" (Romans 6:3). Having been clothed with Him in these baptismal waters (Galatians 3:27), we, too, are now what Jesus is. We are adopted into the family of our heavenly Father. By incorporation into His body through Baptism, we are "sons of God" (Romans 8:14) in this Son. We are "beloved children" (Ephesians 5:1) as Christ is the Beloved. It is "your Father's good pleasure to give you the kingdom" (Luke 12:32), the kingdom of the Son in whom He is well pleased.

These are the reasons that Jesus is baptized. He is baptized not for Himself, but for you. He fulfills your righteousness; He opens heaven for you; He gives you His Holy Spirit; He makes you a beloved son or daughter of God with whom the Father is well pleased. Thanks be to God that by means of the water placed on Jesus that day, we are flooded with all the gifts of heaven!

Conclusion

It has been our goal in this session to look at the baptism of Jesus with 20/20 vision, with one eye on the Old Testament and one eye on the New Testament. What happened at the Jordan River that day was not only a marvelous work of God, but also the fulfillment of many Old Testament promises. What we have seen previewed in the life of Israel is now viewed in the life of the One who is Israel reduced to one. Baptized into Him, we are now participants in who Jesus is and what Jesus did. Over the font on the day you were baptized, God the Father said, "This is My beloved Son, with whom I am well pleased." This is His promise! This is His gift!

Closing Prayer

Lord God, heavenly Father, who at the baptism of our Lord made the water of the Jordan River and all water a rich and salutary washing away of sins, grant that we who are baptized into the body of Jesus may ever share in His life and salvation; through the same Jesus Christ, Your Son, our Lord, who lives and reigns with You and the Holy Spirit, one God, now and forever. Amen.

THE BAPTISM OF JESUS

Not Just Plain Water

Take some time to reflect on the common water themes that have been covered in the sessions thus far. Note three or four key similarities between the various Old Testament stories that involve water. How has water been used? For whom has it been used? Has water been associated primarily with good or bad things, cursing or blessing?

Jordan River: Same Song, Final Verse

The Jordan River is part of the story of Israel herself. Briefly review the history recorded in **Joshua 1–5**. Where had Israel been before **Joshua 1**? What was the nation about to encounter when she crossed over into the land of Canaan? Was this land populated or unpopulated? How would it be possible for them to conquer it (**Joshua 2:9**)?

Israel first had to cross the Jordan before beginning the conquest of Canaan. What time of year was this (**Joshua 3:15**)? Was the river at its high or low point? How did this present even more of a challenge to the nation?

How did the nation cross the Jordan River (**Joshua 3**)? What piece of "holy furniture" was central in the crossing? What purpose did the ark serve in the tabernacle (**Exodus 25:10–22**)? With what does David compare the ark (**1 Chronicles 28:2**)? How is Jesus our new "ark of the covenant"?

Joshua is a Hebrew name that means "Yahweh is salvation." If we wrote "Joshua" in Greek, it would be spelled "Jesus." Thus, our Lord Jesus and Joshua share the same name. This is no mere coincidence. How is Jesus our new and better Joshua? If Joshua led Israel in the conquest of the enemy, who has our new and better Joshua conquered? Whom did He face immediately after He was baptized (**Matthew 4:1–11**)?

John: Priest, Prophet, and Baptizer

Read **Matthew 3:1–6**. John the Baptist was a unique individual. What set John apart? How was he different?

Read **Luke 1:5–25**. John was from a priestly family. In fact, his father, Zechariah, was burning incense and praying in the temple when the angel Gabriel told Zechariah that he would be John's father. A normal priest, however, served at the temple in Jerusalem. Where was John's "temple"? What kind of unusual "vestments" did John wear? What kind of language did John the priest use to describe Jesus **(John 1:29)**? Why was this particularly appropriate for a priest to say?

Read **Luke 1:16–17; 76–79**. John was not only a priest, but also a prophet. As a prophet, what was he to do? With which OT prophet was John compared? Compare **2 Kings 1:8** with **Matthew 3:4**. What outward similarity existed between these two men?

What two foods were evidently central in the diet of John the Baptist **(Matthew 3:4)**? What were locusts associated with in the Old Testament (see **Exodus 10:1–20**)? What was honey associated with in the Old Testament **(Exodus 3:8, 17)**? Out of John's mouth proceeded words that threatened God's judgment against unbelief **(Luke 3:7–9)** as well as promised blessings in the Messiah **(Luke 1:76–79; John 1:29–34)**. How might John's diet be symbolic of the two messages of his preaching?

John's preaching was accompanied by his baptizing. John the Baptist simply means "John the Baptizer." This close link between ministry and water is similar to other OT men. How was water associated with Noah, Moses, and Joshua?

Jesus Puts Himself into the Water

The baptism of Jesus is described in various ways by all four evangelists. Read their accounts in **Matthew 3:13–17; Mark 1:9–11; Luke 3:21–22; John 1:29–34**. What are the unique features of each account? What are the similarities?

Matthew records the hesitancy of John the Baptist when Jesus comes to be baptized by him. What does John say? What is the basis of his protest?

How does Jesus respond to John? Take some time to dwell on the words of Jesus' response.

"Let it be so now," Jesus says **(Matthew 3:15)**. Our Lord focuses on the fact that "now" is the time. Compare this "now-ness" of Jesus' response with the words in **Galatians 4:4** about the "fullness of time."

Jesus concludes, "to fulfill all righteousness" **(verse 15)**. What is righteousness? How does Jesus fulfill all righteousness for all people? To what does Isaiah compare our righteousness **(Isaiah 64:6)**? Read **Romans 4**. By what do we receive the righteousness of God?

Jesus also says "for us" (verse 15). What does Jesus mean by "us"? Does He mean Himself and John? Or does He mean Himself, the Father, and the Spirit?

Is it correct to say that when we see Jesus we actually see God (John 1:18; 14:9)?

Is there anything Jesus did not fulfill for us? Think about how Jesus passed through every stage of our life—from infancy to adulthood—and all the while kept God's Law perfectly. Is the Gospel only that Jesus died and rose for you? How is the life of Jesus also Good News for you?

The Spirit's Dove

Read Genesis 1:1–2. When the Holy Spirit descended upon Jesus, He did so in the form of a dove. Elsewhere in the Bible, the Holy Spirit is described as a dove or as hovering as a dove might do. What is the Spirit doing? Over what is He hovering? Compare this with the baptism of Jesus in light of 2 Corinthians 5:17. Paul says that if we are in Jesus we are a _____ _____. Discuss how the baptism of Jesus is like a re-Genesis of the world.

How many baptisms does Ephesians 4:5–6 say there are? Discuss this statement: "Indeed, you could rightly say that there has really been only one Baptism ever: the baptism of Jesus. Every other Baptism is not a repetition of Jesus', but an incorporation into His."

Read Genesis 8:8–12. What place does the dove have in the account of the Flood and Noah's ark? How is this dove a bearer of good news? What kind of good news? In what way is the Holy Spirit's coming in the form of a dove also good news? From what kind of "flood" are we rescued by being baptized into Jesus (see 2 Peter 3:5–7)?

The Heavenly Veil Is Opened

What happens when Jesus comes out of the Jordan River?

How is the Holy Spirit involved in your Baptism (Titus 3:4–5)? What does your body become when you are baptized (1 Corinthians 3:16; 6:19)?

Compare this miracle with the vision of Ezekiel in Ezekiel 1. What are some similarities? Beside what kind of body of water do both miracles happen? What does Ezekiel see in 1:26–28? What kind of form does God have in this appearance?

The Heavenly Voice

What does the Father say from heaven when Jesus is baptized?

Read **Exodus 20:1–21.** At Jesus' baptism the Father spoke from heaven. At Mount Sinai God also spoke from heaven. What was the people's reaction to God speaking? Compare what God spoke at Sinai with what God spoke at the Jordan River. How are these messages different?

At Sinai God spoke Ten Commandments, the Law. At the Jordan the Father identifies the Son, who came to do what with the Law **(Matthew 5:17)**?

Jesus is the Son of God by nature. He is "God of God, Light of Light, very God of very God." He is the Son of God from all eternity. The Scriptures, however, also refer to the baptized as "sons of God" **(Romans 8:14)**. What image does Paul use in **Galatians 3:27** to describe our close connection to Jesus in Baptism?

Read **Romans 8:15**. There Paul says that we became the sons of God by _____.

Review and discuss the Fourth Chief Part of Luther's Small Catechism. How does the study of Jesus' baptism further help to answer many of the questions in this part of the Catechism?

JESUS AND PETER WALK ON WATER

Lesson Focus

When Jesus walks on the water, our thoughts return to the crossing of the Red Sea. There our Lord rescued Israel, made a path through the sea, and granted His people faith to cross over the water. He ruled over that water, and by that water He drew His church to Himself. He grants us faith in the baptismal font, draws us to Himself, and comforts us amidst our doubts and fears.

Opening Prayer

O Lord God Almighty, who rules over the winds and the waves of the sea, grant us faith in the midst of all our troubles, that living by Your Word, we may receive help and comfort in every time of need; through Jesus Christ, our Lord. Amen.

Master of the Sea

Read the accounts of the storm at sea and Jesus walking on the water in Matthew 14:22–33; Mark 6:45–52; and John 6:16–21. Test your Old Testament ears! See how many possible allusions to events in the life of Israel you can find. List all the key features of the text: crossing the sea, storm, walking on water, and so on. Note key themes in the story, as well as in stories that immediately precede and follow this account.

Anyone who has ever been in a storm at sea has quite a story to tell. The smaller the boat, the bigger the story! Few things are more powerful and destructive than crashing waves and whipping winds, especially when these join together to mount an attack against a ship. No matter how large the vessel, it will take quite a beating before making it back to shore—if it does. The ocean floor is the cemetery of many a boat that never made it back to dry land.

The rough and ready fishermen whom Jesus called as His disciples knew all about the storms that often fell upon the Sea of Galilee. These men were not novices. With their own eyes they had seen the clouds quickly form, and with trembling

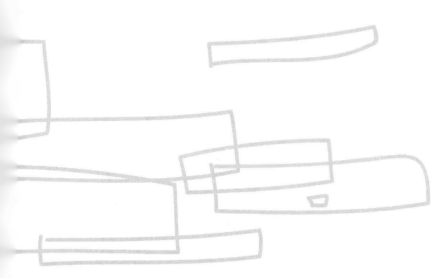

hands they had grabbed for the oars as they felt the waves slap against the sides of their boats. Experienced though they were, they knew that storms had no friends, only enemies. It was fight or be killed. The waves took no prisoners.

All of this is what makes the story of the storm at sea and Jesus walking on the water such a memorable part of the Gospel narrative. Three of the Gospels record this story (Matthew 14:22–33; Mark 6:45–52; John 6:16–21). It is packed with fear, excitement, anticipation, and—finally—blessed calm. The divine power of Jesus and the frail faith of His followers are exhibited for all the world to see.

But there is more to this story than divine muscle and human weakness. It is truly a story of the church—of us—and the Lord who is the church's head and Savior. It is the story of how the Lord teaches his church to live by faith, to forsake all and cling solely to His Word. Finally, it is a story about the God who not only walks on water, but rules water and rules through water. He uses water to create faith in the hearts of His people. He uses water to draw His people to Himself. And He uses

water to show us that He is the Son of God, the Creator, who has come down to the earth (and to the water) to re-create this fallen creation for us and for our salvation.

Feeding of the 5,000

Given some of the imagery in this story, as well as some key themes, which Old Testament story in particular seems to be the backdrop against which we are to understand the crossing of the Sea of Galilee?

When you listen to the stories about water in the Gospels, you hear echoes of other stories. You may not always be able to put your finger on it, but you can sense some kind of connection between accounts such as the Flood and the crossing of the Red Sea and the baptism of Jesus or the storm at sea. Indeed, they share a common kinship. Their roots are closely intertwined. As we have seen in the prior sessions, to try and understand one without comparing it to the others is like trying to understand one piece of a jigsaw puzzle while the other pieces are still in the box. To see the full meaning of an individual story (or sometimes even to get the main point), one must view it in light of the others.

In the Gospel story of the storm at sea and Jesus (along with Peter) walking on the water, there are several allusions to Old Testament stories. Prominent among these is the crossing of the Red Sea (Exodus 14). If you carefully read all three accounts in the Gospels of Matthew, Mark, and John, you will not find any explicit reference back to the exodus. Nowhere does the evangelist write, "The work Jesus performed here is like the work He performed for Israel at the Red Sea." That is simply not the way the evangelists wrote. Their approach is much more subtle, or, at least it seems subtle to us. No doubt the original hearers of these Gospel stories made connections to Old Testament events much more readily than we do. Their ears were simply more attuned to the Old Testament stories than ours are. What they heard in full volume we often hear only as a whisper—if we hear it at all! We are often tone-deaf to what was sweet music to their ears.

Radio stations frequently have contests in which listeners are allowed to hear only a few notes of some song. They then have to name the title of the song, the singer, and so forth. If a listener really knows his music, all he needs to hear is that small snippet for the whole song to be in his head. So it is in the Gospels. All the Israelites needed to hear was a snippet of some Old Testament story—a word, a phrase, or an allusion—and the whole story was in their mind. So how can we pick up on this "sweet music"? How can we begin to hear what they heard so clearly?

A helpful place to begin is by noting the context in which a story occurs. Linking it with the Old Testament stories with which it shares a family resemblance is key. It was no mere coincidence that immediately after Jesus was baptized, the Spirit led Him out into the wilderness where He fasted for 40 days and was tempted by the devil (Matthew 3:13–4:11). The 40 days Jesus spent in the wilderness is like the 40 years Israel spent in the wilderness. And immediately after what incident did Israel

spend those 40 years in the wilderness? Their own "baptism" in the Red Sea!

Israel's Baptism in the Red Sea➡ 40 Years of Testing in the Wilderness

Jesus' Baptism in the Jordan River ➡ 40 Days of Temptation in the Wilderness

If we note the context in which these temptations of Jesus occur, we can more readily understand (at least one of the reasons) why He was tempted—to be faithful in resisting temptation—where Israel was not.

What happens before the disciples get into the boat? Where else in the Bible do we read about large numbers of people being miraculously fed with bread while they were in the wilderness (Exodus 16)? How many baskets of leftovers were there? Of what does this number remind you? In the Gospel of John what happens after the disciples and Jesus cross the Sea of Galilee? What is the subject of this discourse? Discuss how all of these events set the tone for how we are to "hear" the crossing of the Sea of Galilee.

Context is also important in the story of the storm at sea. Especially important is the context that immediately precedes the account of the crossing: the feeding of the 5,000 (Matthew 14:13–21). This miraculous meal is full of allusions to events in the exodus. As the opening music of a larger composition sets the tone for the piece about to be played, so the verses that lead up to verses 22–33 set the "exodus" tone for what is to follow. The miracle of the feeding of the 5,000, especially in John's Gospel (chapter 6), is seen as the fulfillment of the giving of the manna in the wilderness (Exodus 16). In John 6 Jesus is designated the prophet like Moses (John 6:14; Deuteronomy 18:18) and the true bread—the true Manna—out of heaven (John 6:32–33). He feeds the crowds of people with miraculous food, just as Moses (or, more accurately, God) fed the people of Israel. There are 12 baskets of leftover fragments remaining (Matthew 14:20), just as there were 12 tribes in Israel. He feeds them right after

He heals many of the sick, just as the Lord fed Israel manna in the wilderness (Exodus 16) right after He had promised to be Israel's healer (Exodus 15:26). These (and still other!) references to events closely connected with the exodus give us the "ears to hear" the crossing of the Sea of Galilee.

As you prepare to hear the account of the disciples crossing the raging sea, Jesus walking on water, and Peter walking then sinking, hear that account with ears that listen closely for whispers of events in the exodus. In particular, tune your ears to hear similar language, imagery, or themes that are shared by the story of the crossing of the Red Sea and the crossing of the Sea of Galilee.

Praying on a Mountain

Why did Jesus send His disciples ahead of Him in the boat? Could Jesus have been putting His disciples to the test? Does God test His children? Point out some stories from the New Testament or Old Testament where God tested His people (Abraham [Genesis 22:1]; Joseph [Genesis 37; Psalm 105:19]; and Israel [Exodus 15:25]). What is the difference between a test and a temptation? What does James say is the purpose of God's testing (James 1:1–4)? What does God say to St. Paul during his time of testing (2 Corinthians 12:7–10)?

This stormy account begins with relative calm. Jesus fed the multitude with the five loaves of bread and the two fish. The disciples retrieved more leftovers than the food with which they had begun the meal. Then it was time to move on. The evangelist Matthew records what happened next: "Immediately He made the disciples get into the boat and go before Him to the other side, while He dismissed the crowds. And after He had dismissed the crowds, He went up on the mountain by Himself to pray. When evening came, He was there alone" (Matthew 14:22–23).

Although they did not know it, the disciples were about to enter a perilous situation. They were sent into this situation by Jesus Himself. Jesus knew very well that a storm would soon fall upon the Sea of Galilee. But He also knew very well how He would deliver His followers from the storm. His plan was just beginning to unfold, though hidden from the eyes of His disciples.

Why would our Lord send His disciples ahead of Him into a storm? Possibly, that their faith might be tested. The Bible is full of stories where the faith of God's children is put to the test in one way or another. God tested the faith of Abraham by commanding him to offer up Isaac as a sacrifice (Genesis 22:1); Joseph was tested by being sold into slavery by his brothers (Genesis 37; Psalm 105:19); and the nation of Israel was tested by the Lord throughout her 40 years in the wilderness (Exodus 15:25; 16:4; 20:20; Deuteronomy 8:2). Bear in mind that these tests were not temptations. As James says, "Let no one say when he is tempted, 'I am being tempted by God,' for God cannot be tempted with evil, and he himself tempts no one" (James 1:13). When the Lord tests someone, it is not His will that this test lead to evildoing (as with temptations). Rather, it is His will that the test lead a believer to rely more upon Him and His grace. Relying more upon God while simultaneously relying less upon ourselves is always a painful experience. Our sinful nature wants to rely upon no one but itself. We think we can take care of ourselves, make it on our own strength, pull ourselves up by our bootstraps. Thus, when tested, the sinful nature is forced once again under the waters of Baptism. We are led to realize that we truly have no one and nothing but God to help us. Faith grasps Him in His Word. The "new man" in us is raised to living faith in the God who always delivers us in time of need.

But the testing of the disciples' faith is only one reason for the Lord sending His disciples ahead of Him into the storm. In fact, it is the less important reason. The main reason, which we will describe as the session unfolds, is that the Lord might reveal Himself as the Creator who rules over creation for our good and who saves His church in every time of need.

When the disciples get into the boat, where

does Jesus go? Read Exodus 32:11–14. Who else is known for having prayed on a mountain?

Since Jesus is true God, how could He pray? Did He talk to Himself? To whom did He pray (Matthew 26:39, 42; John 17)? What does Hebrews tell us about the prayers of Jesus (5:7)? Is Jesus still praying today (Romans 8:34)? For whom does He pray?

Two verses cited earlier (Matthew 14:22–23) indicate that after the Lord sent His disciples ahead of Him in the boat, He dismissed the crowds and went up on the mountain by Himself to pray. It often strikes people as strange that the Son of God should pray. "Was He praying to Himself?" they sometimes wonder. "After all, Jesus is God, and those who pray, pray to God." No, Jesus did not pray to Himself. He prayed to His Father. He prayed because, although He is fully divine, He is also fully human. And as a human, as a flesh-and-blood man, He prays. He intercedes for those in need. He prays for Himself. He prays for wisdom, guidance, help, and whatever else He needs. The author of Hebrews puts it this way: "In the days of His flesh, Jesus offered up prayers and supplications, with loud cries and tears, to Him who was able to save Him from death, and He was heard because of His reverence" (Hebrews 5:7). In fact, Jesus is *still* praying today, praying for us: "Christ Jesus is the one who died—more than that, who was raised—who is at the right hand of God, who indeed is interceding for us" (Romans 8:34).

As One who prays, who intercedes for us, Jesus is like Moses (or perhaps we should say, "Moses was like Jesus!"). On several occasions we have explicit testimony that Moses prayed for the Israelites (see Exodus 32:11–14; Psalm 106:23). No doubt this intercession was a daily occurrence for Moses. Just as Jesus prayed up on the mountain, Moses was intimately associated with mountains, including the mountain on which He prayed for Israel. He received his call to return to Egypt at Horeb, the region in which Mount Sinai is located (Exodus 3–4); received the Ten Commandments in

the same location, on Mount Sinai (Exodus 20); and died on Mount Nebo as He overlooked the Promised Land (Deuteronomy 34).

Therefore, Jesus sends His disciples ahead of Him on the boat and goes up on the mountain to pray. He no doubt intercedes for them. He prays for their safety, their faith, their endurance during the trial to come. Like Moses before Him, He intercedes for the saints who are also sinners.

A Storm at Sea

What impression do you get of the storm that fell upon the Sea of Galilee as the disciples tried to cross the waters? In Matthew 14:24 and Mark 6:48 words such as *beaten* and *painfully* are used to describe the waves and progress of the boat. Both of these words are formed from the same Greek word used in Revelation 20:10 to describe the tortures of hell. This was truly a "hellish" storm!

As Jesus prayed to His Father that night on the mountain, down below on the Sea of Galilee the disciples were facing what many a sailor had faced on these waters: a violent storm. The evangelists who record this story use language that clearly communicates the intensity of the wind and waves.

When evening came, [Jesus] was there alone, but the boat by this time was a long way from the land, beaten by the waves, for the wind was against them. (Matthew 14:23–24)

And when evening came the boat was out on the sea, and [Jesus] was alone on the land. And He saw that they were making headway painfully, for the wind was against them. (Mark 6:47–48)

When evening came, His disciples went down to the sea, got into a boat, and started across the sea to Capernaum. It was now dark, and Jesus had not yet come to them. The sea became rough because a strong wind was blowing. (John 6:16–18)

One thing is clear from each of these three accounts: this was not an easy voyage! In fact, one of the Greek words used by Matthew and Mark tells us that this was literally a tortuous journey. The boat was "beaten [literally, 'tortured'] by the waves" (Matthew 14:24). Jesus "saw that they were making headway painfully [literally, 'tortuously']" (Mark 6:48). This same Greek word is used elsewhere to describe the torment of hell (Revelation 20:10). One gets the distinct impression that the disciples were in quite a "hellish" storm.

Note some parallel themes between the Israelites' crossing of the Red Sea (Exodus 14) and the disciples' crossing of the Sea of Galilee. How was God involved in putting them into the situation (Exodus 14:1–4; Matthew 14:22)? What role does water play? Is it friend or foe? What kind of faith is exhibited? Is it strong or weak? What is said about fear (Exodus 14:13; Matthew 14:27)? What is the final outcome of the story?

The predicament of the disciples is, on the surface, not exactly like that of the Israelites who were caught at the Red Sea, but the situations do have some similarities. To begin with, in John's Gospel the account is both preceded by and followed by events that point us back to the exodus. John first records the feeding of the 5,000 (John 6:1–15), in which the people recognize Jesus to be "the Prophet [like Moses] who is to come into the world!" (John 6:14; Deuteronomy 18:15). Then he describes the crossing of the sea (John 6:16–21). Afterward, John records the sermon of Jesus in which He points to Himself as the true Manna, the bread that comes down from heaven (John 6:22–59). This order of events is like the order of the Book of Exodus itself: First, Moses the prophet is sent to Israel (Exodus 4–13); second, Israel crosses the Red Sea (Exodus 14–15); third, God gives manna to the people (Exodus 16).

Not only is the order of events similar, there are thematic links between the accounts as well:

In both cases God placed His people into a situation in which their faith is tested. Just as Jesus sent His disciples onto the sea, so He sent Israel to camp at the Red Sea (Exodus 14:1–4). In both situations, their eyes would see only impending disaster. The ears of their hearts, however, were to hear and cling to the Word of the Father. Instead of trusting in their own strength or willpower, they were to rely on their good and gracious Lord, who had bound Himself to them in His Word.

* In both these cases water seems to be the enemy. The water of the Red Sea blocked the path of escape for the Israelites. The water of the Sea of Galilee threatened to become the liquid grave of the disciples.

* Sadly, in both cases the people exhibit less than exemplary faith. When the Israelites realized that the Egyptians were closing in on them, they verbally attacked Moses, accusing him of leading them out into the wilderness to kill them (Exodus 14:11–12). Likewise, although Peter at first demonstrated faith in leaving the boat to walk on the water toward Jesus, he quickly became frightened and began to sink. The words of Jesus to Peter are applicable to all the disciples: "O you of little faith, why did you doubt?" (Matthew 14:31).

* In both of these situations fear and faith strove for the upper hand. The Lord spoke His Word of comfort to His people, beginning with words that admonished them to stop being afraid. Through Moses the Lord said to the Israelites, "Fear not, stand firm, and see the salvation of the LORD, which He will work for you today" (Exodus 14:13). To His disciples, who thought they were seeing a ghost when Jesus approached their boat, our Lord said, "Take heart; it is I. Do not be afraid" (Matthew 14:27).

We can see that in both these stories the hand of God is at work. He is preparing His people to see that in Him alone is their salvation; in Him alone is their hope; by Him alone will they be brought through the time of testing.

Jesus Walking on Water

How do people sometimes use the phrase "walking on water" in everyday speech? What kind of action do these words describe?

Read Matthew 14:33. What is the reaction of the disciples when Jesus finally gets in the boat? What does this action of Jesus tell the

disciples about His identity?

The story of Jesus walking on the water is one of the best-known incidents in His life. In fact, it is so well-known that the action of walking on water is equated with superhuman abilities. If an employee is asked by his boss to fix a difficult problem, he might reply in frustration, "Good grief! I can't walk on water!" The implication is that walking on water is beyond our ordinary ability. It is miraculous, and, therefore, a divine action.

It is certainly true that walking on water is a miraculous, divine action. When Jesus walked on water, He demonstrated to His disciples that He was true God. Indeed, when Jesus gets into the boat, His awestruck disciples confess, "Truly You are the Son of God" (Matthew 14:33).

One might ask, though, if that is the only point—or even the *main* point—of the miracle: to prove that Jesus is fully divine? Is more implied than this? To answer such questions, we need to think about the situation in which this miracle takes place, as well as any Old Testament background that might help us.

First, consider the obvious fact that this takes place on water, and not just water, but on a storm-tossed sea. Jesus could very well have walked on air, should He have chosen to. He could have walked on calm water. But He did not. He treads over waves in the stormy waters of the sea.

Second, let us ask if there is any Old Testament background that might help us to understand the significance of the fact that Jesus walks where and when He does. A few OT texts shed light on this.

When Jesus walked on the water, He clearly showed that He was God. What else did He demonstrate? Read the following Old Testament texts and discuss them in light of the story from the Gospels.

Psalm 77: How might these words have been an appropriate prayer for the disciples while in the boat? In Psalm 77:10–12 what does the psalmist say he will do? On which "mighty deeds" does he meditate in verses 13–20? What kind of picture does this give of God?

What does He do in the sea? How does this relate to the story in the Gospels?

Job 9:1–10: How is God described in these verses? How does He relate to creation? If one views the crossing of the sea through the lens of 9:8, how does this give a clearer picture of what Jesus was doing?

Isaiah 43:16–21: What Old Testament event is described in verses 16–17? If this event is one of the "former things" (verse 18), then what is the "new thing" (verse 19) that God will do? Relate verse 16 to Matthew 14.

The first of these texts is Psalm 77. This psalm is remarkably fitting for the storm at sea. The first nine verses describe a great suffering that has befallen someone. In his affliction the psalmist wonders if God has rejected him, if God has forgotten to be gracious. This sounds as if it could have come from the lips of the disciples as they wrestled the waves that night in Galilee! Verses 10–12 introduce what the psalmist considers to be the answer to his plight. He will "remember the deeds of the LORD," God's "wonders of old," His "mighty deeds." In verses 13–20 we learn that the "mighty deeds" on which the psalmist meditates occur when God brought Israel through the Red Sea. The psalm ends with these words: "Your way was through the sea, Your path through the great waters; yet Your footprints were unseen. You led Your people like a flock by the hand of Moses and Aaron" (Psalm 77:19–20). The Lord is pictured as a shepherd with two under-shepherds—Moses and Aaron. God was walking with "footprints . . . unseen" down the path that He has made in the waters. As He does so, He leads His people to safety. The psalm ends with no reference to the suffering that the psalmist described in the first nine verses. The implication, however, is obvious—the psalmist was comforted in his affliction by meditation on the saving action of God in the crossing of the Red Sea. Just as God has walked His people through the Red Sea, so He would walk the psalmist through his path of suffering.

When one links this psalm with the account of

the storm, the connections are very illuminating. When Jesus comes walking on the water to His disciples, He is saying more than simply, "Hey, guys, look at Me—I'm God!" He is saying, "Behold, I am the One who walked with footprints unseen through the Red Sea; I am the One who helps the psalmist of Psalm 77; and I am the One who has come to help you, O storm-tossed disciples. I am none other than the Lord, the God of Israel."

Job laments that the all-powerful God is so much greater than man that "if one wished to contend with Him, one could not answer Him once in a thousand times" (9:3). He "removes mountains . . . shakes the earth . . . commands the sun . . . and trampled the waves of the sea" (9:5–8). God is pictured not only as Creator, but as the Creator who remains in control of His creation. He who made all things still rules all things. Creation is literally beneath His feet. When Jesus walked on water, when He "trampled the waves of the sea," He was letting His disciples (and us) know that He is the God of Job, the God who rules creation, the God who rules that creation for our good. Although He is all-powerful, He is the God who looks down in pity upon His children in their distress, such as Job, and rescues them (Job 42).

In Isaiah 43 the prophet Isaiah contrasts the former exodus with a new exodus that God will accomplish for His exiled people. This is a very common theme in Isaiah and several other Old Testament prophets (Jeremiah and Hosea, in particular). The prophet says:

Thus says the LORD, who makes a way in the sea, a path in the mighty waters, who brings forth chariot and horse, army and warrior; they lie down, they cannot rise, they are extinguished, quenched like a wick: "Remember not the former things, nor consider the things of old. Behold, I am doing a new thing; now it springs forth, do you not perceive it? I will make a way in the wilderness and rivers in the desert. The wild beasts will honor me, the jackals and the ostriches, for I give water in the wilderness, rivers in the desert, to give drink to My chosen people, the people whom I formed for Myself that they might declare My praise." (Isaiah 43:16–21)

The "former things," such as "mak[ing] a way in the sea" and bringing down "chariot and horse, army and warrior," are the things of the first exodus. At that time, God made "a way in the sea" by opening up the Red Sea so His people could pass through, but bringing the waters back to destroy the chariots, horses, army, and warriors of Egypt. Now, God says, He is planning to do something new, something better. Rather than making a way through the water, He will "make a way in the wilderness and rivers in the desert" (43:19). This portrays the salvation God will give us in the Messiah. We sinners are pictured as exiled from God in distant lands. God, however, will not leave us in slavery. He sends His Son, His Anointed One, to bring us back to Himself. As we cross the wilderness of this world, to journey back to Him, He makes a way for us to travel and gives us drink in the desert. The link from this section of Isaiah with the Gospel story of Jesus walking on water occurs in verse 16. As in Psalm 77, the action of walking on water is seen as indicative not only of a divine action, but of an action accomplished by the God of Israel, the true God, who rescues His people. Every step Jesus took on the sea that night punctuated this truth. Just as the Lord transformed the Red Sea into a pathway for His feet to lead His flock safely across from slavery to freedom, so He makes the Sea of Galilee a pathway for His feet to meet His flock in the midst of the waters and lead them from peril to safety.

We often say that actions speak louder than words. In light of the three Old Testament texts you just studied, what are the actions of Jesus saying? With whom is He identified?

When Jesus walks on the sea He is saying much more than simply, "I am divine." He is saying, "I am the God of Abraham, Isaac, and Jacob. I am Yahweh. I am He who led the children of Israel through the Red Sea on dry ground. I am He who destroyed their enemies in the same sea. I am He who rules over the wind and the waves. And I am He who will rescue you, O disciples, O church, from all the enemies that face you. I am with you to deliver you."

Walking and Sinking Peter

Read Matthew 14:26. How do the disciples react when they see Jesus? How does Jesus respond?

As is often the case, when something extraordinary happens, the significance of it is not immediately grasped by the onlookers. At times in the Scriptures when something extraordinary or miraculous occurs, the significance is not grasped for a long time. Many of the events in the life of Jesus, in particular, were misunderstood or misconstrued until after His resurrection, ascension, and the coming of the Holy Spirit. One need only read about His disciples' reaction to the crucifixion to see this (Luke 24:13–24). Such was the case also when Jesus walked on water. When the disciples saw Him, they did not exclaim, "Look, there is Jesus, showing us that He is the God of Israel by walking on water!" Hardly! Rather, they were terrified and cried out, "It is a ghost!" (Matthew 14:26). Jesus, however, calmed their fears, saying, "Take heart; it is I. Do not be afraid" (14:27).

Why does Peter get out of the boat? In this action Jesus drew Peter to Himself on the water. How might we relate this action to Holy Baptism?

What caused Peter to become frightened (14:30)? What was Jesus' response (14:31)? What does the word *immediately* tell you about Jesus?

Peter began to grasp the significance of Jesus' actions. He said, "'Lord, if it is You, command me to come to You on the water.' [Jesus] said, 'Come.' So Peter got out of the boat and walked on the water and came to Jesus" (Matthew 14:28–29). What was Peter thinking? Why would he make such a request? For one thing, Peter was asking for divine confirmation of this sign. He wanted to make sure that this was truly Jesus. Moreover, it is clear that Peter also wished to be with his Lord. In the midst of the wind, the waves, and his own fear, Peter knew that the place to be was with Christ. Jesus drew Peter to Himself on the water. He granted this disciple faith to leave the boat, to tread the waves, and to come to Him. Now this is a miracle, indeed! One wonders, in fact, which is the greater miracle: Jesus walking on water or Peter leaving the boat to walk on water!

One is tempted at this point to jump right to the next scene, when Peter begins to sink. But there's no need to rush. Ponder how truly miraculous the gift of faith is, even when that faith is small (Matthew 14:31). Peter walking on water reminds one of another verse from Isaiah, where the Lord says:

> Fear not, for I have redeemed you; I have called you by name, you are Mine. When you pass through the waters, I will be with you; and through the rivers, they shall not overwhelm you; when you walk through fire you shall not be burned, and the flame shall not consume you. For I am the LORD your God, the Holy One of Israel, your Savior. (Isaiah 43:1–3)

Atop that stormy sea Peter was safe, for the Lord was with him. In the midst of these tumultuous waters, Peter was given faith—no matter how big or little it was—to cling to the Holy One of Israel, his Savior.

It is not really that different in the church today. God still works faith in the hearts of His people in the midst of water. He still draws people to Himself on the water. The baptismal font is like the Sea of Galilee. In that font stands our Lord. He is present there just as He was at the Red Sea, just as He was at the Sea of Galilee, to rescue His people, to work faith in their hearts, to save them from destruction, and to bring them to Himself. By His Word Jesus granted Peter faith to come to Him over the water. So it is in the church. By His Word spoken over the water of Baptism, Jesus draws people to Himself. Through His Word Jesus grants faith to the youngest of infants and the oldest of adults. Each of us is "Peter" in the font. We come over the water to Jesus. We are safe with Him.

Of course, the story continues. It records the feebleness of Peter's faith. "When he saw the wind, he was afraid, and beginning to sink he cried out,

'Lord, save me.' Jesus immediately reached out His hand and took hold of him, saying to him, 'O you of little faith, why did you doubt?' And when they got into the boat, the wind ceased" (Matthew 14:30–32). The tendency here is simply to concentrate on the "little faith" of Peter. But to do so is a mistake. Rather than focusing on the smallness of faith, we ought to focus on the largeness of our Lord's compassion. Note, in particular, that word that is easily overlooked: *immediately* (Matthew 14:31). Our loving Lord "*immediately* reached out His hand." He did not let Peter flail about in the water, giving him a tongue-lashing for having such a miniscule faith. Instantly, Jesus came to His rescue. To be sure, He lamented Peter's doubt, but Peter's doubt did not affect our Lord's care and compassion.

How do we also exhibit lack of faith or weakness of faith? How is the prayer of the father in Mark 9:24 the prayer of us all? What promise does God make in Psalm 50:15?

What great comfort this is to us! All of us can echo in our own prayers the petition of another man in the Gospels, "Lord, I believe; help Thou mine unbelief" (Mark 9:24 KJV). Not one of us has perfect faith. We all have doubts. We all have fears. We all are a mixed bag of belief and unbelief, fear and faith, trust and doubt. We are all, in other words, sinners and saints simultaneously. But no matter how strong or weak, how big or little our faith may be, we have our whole Lord. A little faith does not have a little Jesus. Faith receives Christ, the whole Christ, the God of love, care, concern, and compassion. When we, like Peter, are sinking in our own doubts and fears, there is the hand of Jesus, reaching out to save us.

Conclusion

When Jesus walks on the water, our thoughts return to the crossing of the Red Sea. There our Lord rescued Israel, made a path through the sea, and granted His people faith to cross over the water. He ruled over that water, and by that water He drew His church to Himself. So it was at the Sea of Galilee, and so it is in our own lives. Jesus is none other than the Lord God of Israel, the God of Abraham, Isaac, and Jacob, the God who through water saves us from the threatening perils of our sins. In the baptismal font, He grants us faith, draws us to Himself, and comforts us amidst our doubts and fears. Thanks be to the Lord Jesus Christ, the God who rules over the water for our good, for our life, and for our salvation.

Closing Prayer

Almighty God, because You know that we of ourselves have no strength, keep us both outwardly and inwardly that we may be defended from all adversities that may happen to the body and from all evil thoughts that may assault and hurt the soul; through Jesus Christ, Your Son, our Lord, who lives and reigns with You and the Holy Spirit, one God, now and forever. Amen (Collect for the Third Sunday in Lent, *Lutheran Worship*, p. 36).

Jesus and Peter Walk on Water

Master of the Sea

Read the accounts of the storm at sea and Jesus walking on the water in **Matthew 14:22–33; Mark 6:45–52;** and **John 6:16–21.** Test your Old Testament ears! See how many possible allusions to events in the life of Israel you can find. List all the key features of the text: crossing the sea, storm, walking on water, and so on. Note key themes in the story, as well as in stories that immediately precede and follow this account.

Feeding of the 5,000

Given some of the imagery in this story, as well as some key themes, which Old Testament story in particular seems to be the backdrop against which we are to understand the crossing of the Sea of Galilee?

What happens before the disciples get into the boat? Where else in the Bible do we read about large numbers of people being miraculously fed with bread while they were in the wilderness **(Exodus 16)**? How many baskets of leftovers were there? Of what does this number remind you? In the Gospel of John what happens after the disciples and Jesus cross the Sea of Galilee? What is the subject of this discourse? Discuss how all of these events set the tone for how we are to "hear" the crossing of the Sea of Galilee.

Praying on a Mountain

Why did Jesus send His disciples ahead of Him in the boat? Could Jesus have been putting His disciples to the test? Does God test His children? Point out some stories from the New Testament or Old Testament where God tested His people (Abraham **[Genesis 22:1]**; Joseph **[Genesis 37; Psalm 105:19]**; and Israel **[Exodus 15:25]**). What is the difference between a test and a temptation? What does James say is the purpose of God's testing **(James 1:1–4)**? What does God say to St. Paul during his time of testing **(2 Corinthians 12:7–10)**?

When the disciples get into the boat, where does Jesus go? Read **Exodus 32:11–14.** Who else is known for having prayed on a mountain?

Since Jesus is true God, how could He pray? Did He talk to Himself? To whom did He pray **(Matthew 26:39, 42; John 17)**? What does Hebrews tell us about the prayers of Jesus **(5:7)**? Is Jesus still praying today **(Romans 8:34)**? For whom does He pray?

A Storm at Sea

What impression do you get of the storm that fell upon the Sea of Galilee as the disciples tried to cross the waters? In **Matthew 14:24** and **Mark 6:48** words such as *beaten* and *painfully* are used to describe the waves and progress of the boat. Both of these words are formed from the same Greek word used in **Revelation 20:10** to describe the tortures of hell. This was truly a "hellish" storm!

Note some parallel themes between the Israelites' crossing of the Red Sea **(Exodus 14)** and the disciples' crossing of the Sea of Galilee. How was God involved in putting them into the situation **(Exodus 14:1–4; Matthew 14:22)**? What role does water play? Is it friend or foe? What kind of faith is exhibited? Is it strong or weak? What is said about fear **(Exodus 14:13; Matthew 14:27)**? What is the final outcome of the story?

Jesus Walking on Water

How do people sometimes use the phrase "walking on water" in everyday speech? What kind of action do these words describe?

Read **Matthew 14:33**. What is the reaction of the disciples when Jesus finally gets in the boat? What does this action of Jesus tell the disciples about His identity?

When Jesus walked on the water, He clearly showed that He was God. What else did He demonstrate? Read the following Old Testament texts and discuss them in light of the story from the Gospels.

Psalm 77: How might these words have been an appropriate prayer for the disciples while in the boat? In **Psalm 77:10–12** what does the psalmist say he will do? On which "mighty deeds" does he meditate in **verses 13–20**? What kind of picture does this give of God? What does He do in the sea? How does this relate to the story in the Gospels?

Job 9:1–10: How is God described in these verses? How does He relate to creation? If one views the crossing of the sea through the lens of **9:8,** how does this give a clearer picture of what Jesus was doing?

Isaiah 43:16–21: What Old Testament event is described in **verses 16–17**? If this event is one of the "former things" **(verse 18)**, then what is the "new thing" **(verse 19)** that God will do? Relate **verse 16** to **Matthew 14.**

We often say that actions speak louder than words. In light of the three Old Testament texts you just studied, what are the actions of Jesus saying? With whom is He identified?

Walking and Sinking Peter

Read **Matthew 14:26.** How do the disciples react when they see Jesus? How does Jesus respond?

Why does Peter get out of the boat? In this action Jesus drew Peter to Himself on the water. How might we relate this action to Holy Baptism?

What caused Peter to become frightened **(14:30)**? What was Jesus' response **(14:31)**? What does the one word *immediately* tell you about Jesus?

How do we also exhibit lack of faith or weakness of faith? How is the prayer of the father in **Mark 9:24** the prayer of us all? What promise does God make in **Psalm 50:15**?